more
than a meal

PRODUCED BY

THE MUMS' GROUP ST. GEORGE'S CHURCH, LEEDS

EDITED BY

DAVID F. GOLDSPINK
&
KAY L. GILLOTT

FRONT COVER ARTWORK "THE FISH" 1995 COURTESY & COPYRIGHT OF DAVID HOCKNEY

FOOD PHOTOGRAPHY BY, & COPYRIGHT OF, PAUL HIGGINS & ANDREW WALTON-VAINES

DESIGN & LAYOUT BY EMMA GARRY

© ST. GEORGE'S CHURCH & CRYPT, LEEDS 1998

ISBN 0-9534464-0-9

the moral right of the authors has been asserted.

'THE FISH' 1995 COURTESY AND COPYRIGHT OF DAVID HOCKNEY

DESIGN AND LAYOUT BY EMMA GARRY

FOOD PHOTOGRAPHY BY, AND COPYRIGHT OF, PAUL HIGGINS & ANDREW WALTON-VAINES

FOOD PREPARATION BY GRAEME BARKER AND STEVE CHESNUTT (EXECUTIVE HEAD CHEF AT THE BOAR'S HEAD RESTAURANT, RIPLEY CASTLE, YORKSHIRE)

AND MEMBERS OF THE MUMS' GROUP OF ST. GEORGE'S CHURCH.

PRINTED AND BOUND IN GREAT BRITAIN BY WATMOUGHS CORPORATE PRINT, BRADFORD.

every effort has been made to trace the copyright holders for specific recipes. if any
have been inadvertently overlooked, we will be pleased to make the necessary
arrangements at the first opportunity.

CONTENTS

CHEFS' MENUS FOR SPECIAL OCCASIONS

"AS SOMEONE WHO TRIES HIS HAND IN THE KITCHEN FROM TIME TO TIME (I'M A DAB HAND AT GRAVY!) I'M DELIGHTED TO COMMEND TO YOU THIS WONDERFUL COOKBOOK - AS WELL AS THE WORK OF ST. GEORGE'S CRYPT. THEIR PROGRAMMES WITH THE DISADVANTAGED IN OUR SOCIETY DESERVE YOUR SUPPORT."

SIR CLIFF RICHARD OBE -
PATRON OF THE 'MORE THAN A ROOF APPEAL', ST. GEORGE'S CRYPT, LEEDS

Five members of the mum's group of St. George's Church

Left to right :

Judith Shalkowski

Gillian Smith

Angela Wright

Pauline Nelson

Vivienne Clarke

"Lord, when did we ever see you hungry and feed you?...."

"....Whatever you did for one of the least of these my brothers,

you did for me."

Matthew 25: 37 & 40

INTRODUCTION

Gathering around a table to share a meal with our families or friends is a simple yet tremendously important ritual of daily life, for it provides us with the absolute necessities for our survival, and has the potential to do much more. If the meal looks, smells and tastes delicious, and if it is enjoyed in the company of people who value us, it becomes a feast for the senses and a nourishment to the spirit as well. As the cooks who make this possible, we should feel inspired by the creative potential of our role.

Yet for most of us, standing in our kitchens at 5 o'clock with brains starved of inspiration and families clamouring to be fed, any excitement we might once have felt about cooking seems long gone.

'More Than A Meal' aims to restore that excitement in several ways. It offers new ideas for cooks tired of preparing the same old things, recipes for nutritious meals which can be prepared on a low budget, as well as the favourite recipes of more than 60 well-known celebrities from all walks of life who, identifying with the plight of the homeless, have kindly provided an interesting mix of unusual, serious and lighthearted recipes. Many have added brief comments or shared the memories behind their choice of a particular dish. Our children might soon be asking, not "what's for dinner tonight?" but "whose dinner is it tonight?". For the truly special occasion, professional chefs from across the UK have offered complete menus, inspiring us to create meals as beautiful as they are delicious.

Yet, as its name suggests, 'More Than A Meal' is about more than just food. It is about shelter, or more precisely the loss of shelter, which is the daily experience of the many individuals and families who fall into the category of 'the homeless'. This book aims to remind us of the need, the hopes and the dignity of these people, by offering a glimpse into the lives of people who visit or work at St. George's Crypt in Leeds.

The Crypt of St. George's Church was cleared in 1930 to provide space to care for unemployed homeless people and poverty-stricken families. Sadly, 68 years later, despite the advent of the Welfare State, the work of this charity is needed now as much as ever.

The value of the work at St. George's Crypt is born of the simple belief that everyone needs to be loved and appreciated. This book in turn was born out of appreciation for what the Crypt does. We (see photograph opposite) are all members of the St George's Church Mums' Group. With 15 children between us, we are familiar with the daily chore of sustaining our families' nutritional requirements for a healthy balanced diet. Our initial plan - to swap recipes and raise a little money for the Crypt in the process - grew into a recipe swap on a grand scale, through which many individuals have demonstrated a desire to make a difference in the lives of homeless people.

You too have made a difference, by buying this book and thereby contributing to the redevelopment of the Crypt building. You can continue to help, by contributing towards the £0.5 million running costs of St. George's Crypt, or by supporting similar work in your own community.

This has been a tremendously exciting project on which to work. Like cooks preparing a banquet, we have mixed an abundance of ingredients into the initial small idea: Deadline panic, lots of laughter, sleepless nights, conversations with celebrities and with the homeless, and many prayers. Our hope is that in reading and using 'More Than A Meal' you will catch some of that excitement. It might be that the recipes themselves will inspire you in your cooking; it might just be that you have fun planning, say, a political menu: John Major's risotto followed by Tony Blair's chocolate cake. Or it might be that you see afresh how good it is to share a meal - or more than a meal - with someone else.

ACKNOWLEDGEMENTS

We wish to express our gratitude to the many people who have assisted in the production of this cookbook.

We thank David Hockney for kindly giving us permission to use 'The Fish' 1995 (copyright David Hockney) to produce a cover with a difference.

We are extremely grateful to the professional chefs for their special 3 course menus and the many celebrities from all walks of life who so willingly entered into the spirit and aims of this cookbook by sharing their favourite recipes with us all.

Our thanks also go to Paul Higgins and Andrew Walton-Vaines of the Bradford and Ilkley Community College for their photographic skills, Steve Chesnutt and Graeme Barker for cooking the photographed dishes, Emma Garry for her design work; all given free of charge towards this worthy cause. Joanne Dodd, Judith Greaves, David Barker and Paul Wood (of Watmoughs Corporate Print) also gave of their valuable time and talents to assist in various ways. We also acknowledge, with thanks, sponsorship from Marks and Spencer, The Asda Foundation, Costco and Tupperware.

Kay Gillott and Phil and Debbie Whitehead have spent countless hours, typing, proof-reading and keeping track of endless pieces of paper, along with Nessie Bell's administrative support. To these, together with the staff and clients of St. George's Crypt, and our families and friends who tested the recipes and provided child care and understanding, we say "thank you".

Finally, a huge thank you to David Goldspink, without whose inspiration and efforts this project would never have got off the ground.

St. George's Crypt, Leeds
(Charity No. 250016)

For 68 years our Charity has served the nation by offering hope and physical and spiritual support to homeless individuals (16-80 years old) and low-income families. All who turn to us for help are accepted and treated with respect, regardless of their age, gender, colour or beliefs.

More than 35,700 requests for help were handled during 1997. Through our 3 Hostels and Night Shelter, Emergency and Family Centres we provide an unusually wide range of service provisions, offered 365 days a year. These cost us over £0.5 million.

A life reclaimed from homelessness - and alcohol abuse.

After nearly 7 decades the Crypt building requires major restructuring at a cost of over £1.2 million, hence, our "More Than A Roof" project and appeal. This redevelopment work is essential to comply with Health, Safety and Fire regulations and provide us with a flexibly designed building to respond to the changing demands of society in the 21st Century.

A Grace

Let our hearts be glad

as we gather together.

Let our homes be ready

to welcome the stranger.

Let this food be blessed

as it is shared.

Amen.

SOUPS, SALADS
& STARTERS

NO: 01] CREAM OF BROCCOLI SOUP - *with no cream*

JIMMY CARTER
PRESIDENT OF THE USA 1977-1981 AND WORKER FOR
HABITAT FOR HUMANITY

INGREDIENTS

1 medium onion, chopped

1 clove garlic, crushed

1 tablespoon sunflower oil, or other vegetable oil

1 bay leaf

450 g (1 lb) green broccoli, chopped

625 ml (22 fl oz) light vegetable stock (or broth made with vegetable or chicken bouillon)

1 small potato, chopped (for thickening)

Salt and pepper, to taste

Juice of half a lemon

Low fat plain yoghurt (or sour cream, if you're not watching calories or cholesterol)

METHOD

Place the oil in a large saucepan (or spray the pan with aerosol cooking oil) and sauté the onion and garlic with the bay leaf until soft for 3-4 minutes. Add the broccoli, potato and stock to the pan, cover and simmer gently for 10 minutes. The broccoli should be tender but still bright green. Remove the bay leaf and let the ingredients cool a little.

Transfer all the ingredients into a blender and mix to a not-too uniform purée. If you prefer a thinner soup add some milk at this stage. Season to taste and add the lemon juice. It may need re-heating in a clean pan before serving.

Add a dollop of yoghurt just before serving.

SERVES 4

NO: 02] SPINACH SOUP

TERRY WAITE

WRITER & FORMER ADVISER & ENVOY TO THE
ARCHBISHOP OF CANTERBURY

*"Why did I choose this recipe? Well, I only like spinach in two ways.
One is as a raw spinach salad and the other is in soup."*

INGREDIENTS

1 tablespoon olive oil

1 medium onion, diced

1 small/medium potato

250 g (9 oz) fresh spinach

1 vegetable Oxo cube

850 ml (1^1/2 pints) warm water

Salt and pepper, and if you like it, a dash or so of tabasco sauce

METHOD

Heat the olive oil in a large pan and sauté the diced onion. Dissolve the stock cube in the warm water. When the onion is lightly cooked add the spinach and pour the stock into the pan. Simmer for a while. Boil the potato in its skin or bake in the microwave until soft. Dice the potato, skin and all, and add to the soup. (This will give it a little body and it is better than flour.)

When all is cooked, place the mixture in a blender and give it a good twirl. Return the liquid to the pan again and simmer gently. (If you like cream you can add a little now but it is not really necessary.) Flavour with salt and pepper and tabasco (optional).

The soup is a lovely green colour and would be a wonderful soup for St. Patrick's Day. It is also good for the children, just look what spinach did for Popeye!

SERVES 4

> **ARE YOU AWARE?** APPROXIMATELY 30% OF ALL HOMELESS MEN
> AND WOMEN ARE AGED 16-21.

NO: 03] SOUP FOR ALL SEASONS

MRS BILLY GRAHAM
WIFE OF THE INTERNATIONAL EVANGELIST & WRITER

"Garnish, if desired, with finely blanched carrots and courgettes, or fresh croutons, or a dessertspoon of fresh cream."

INGREDIENTS

1 small onion, chopped

1 garlic clove, minced

2 small leeks, trimmed and well washed

2 medium-sized potatoes, peeled and diced

900 g (2 lb) very ripe tomatoes, skinned and chopped

4 tablespoons butter

2 teaspoons curry powder (optional)

1 bay leaf

1 litre (1¾ pints) chicken stock

Salt and freshly ground black pepper, to taste

250 ml (9 fl oz) double cream, or milk

1 tablespoon chopped parsley, optional

METHOD

Prepare the onions, garlic, leeks and potatoes. Heat the butter in a deep pan. Gently sauté the vegetables over a low heat for about 5 minutes until soft and golden (not brown). Add the prepared tomatoes, curry powder, bay leaf, stock, salt and pepper. Cover and cook over a low heat for about 30 minutes. Remove from the heat and cool slightly. Remove the bay leaf and run the mixture through a blender, adding cream with each batch. If desired, stir in the parsley.

This can be eaten hot or cold.

As an alternative, carrots, broccoli, spinach or cauliflower can be substituted for the tomatoes.

SERVES 6

NO: 04] LENTIL SOUP

GLENDA JACKSON
ACTRESS & MP

INGREDIENTS

25 g (1 oz) butter
1 onion, chopped
2 garlic cloves, crushed
1 tomato, chopped
225 g (8 oz) red lentils
1¼ litre (2 pints) chicken stock
1 teaspoon ground cumin
Salt and freshly ground black pepper, to taste
A dash of lemon juice

METHOD

Melt the butter in a large saucepan, add the onion and garlic and sauté for 5 minutes, until soft. Add the tomato and cook for 1 minute. Wash the lentils and add to the pan with the stock. Bring to the boil and simmer for 30-45 minutes, until the lentils are soft. Allow to cool a little.

Purée in a food processor or blender (but not if a more chunky soup is required) and return to the pan.

Re-heat gently. Add the cumin and season to taste. Stir well and add a dash of lemon juice before serving.

SERVES 4

NO: 05] NAPLES SOUP

JUDITH JACKSON
ST. GEORGE'S CHURCH, LEEDS

INGREDIENTS

2 tablespoons oil
Salt and pepper, to taste
2 small onions, peeled and chopped
2 medium carrots, peeled and chopped
1 medium potato, peeled and cubed
1/4 small white cabbage, chopped
13/4 litres (3 pints) chicken stock
1 rounded tablespoon tomato purée
175 g (6 oz) small pasta shells
110 g (4 oz) peas
4-6 slices bacon, cut up and trimmed of fat
Parmesan cheese, grated, to serve

METHOD

Heat the oil in a saucepan, sauté the onion, the bacon and then the rest of the vegetables (except the peas) all together for 2-3 minutes. Add the stock and tomato purée. Season to taste. Simmer for 1 hour (or 4 hours in a slow cooker). Twenty minutes before serving, cook the pasta and peas, then add to the soup.

Sprinkle with Parmesan cheese. Serve with hot crusty bread.

SERVES 6

NO: 06] CARROT & ORANGE SOUP

EILEEN PICKUP
ST. GEORGE'S CHURCH, LEEDS

INGREDIENTS

450 g (1 lb) carrots, sliced

2 large onions, finely chopped

50 g (2 oz) butter

570 ml (1 pint) chicken or vegetable stock

1 teaspoon of herbs of your choice

Salt and pepper, to taste

2 bay leaves

275 ml (10 fl oz) fresh orange juice

1/4 teaspoon nutmeg or ginger

Mint or parsley sprig to garnish

METHOD

Melt the butter in a saucepan and sauté the onion and carrots for 5 minutes. Add the stock, salt and bay leaves and cook for 20 minutes until the carrots are soft. Remove the bay leaves and mash or liquidise.

Add the orange juice and re-heat gently, with a seasoning of nutmeg or ginger, herbs, and salt and pepper to taste.

Garnish with parsley or mint and serve hot.

SERVES 4-6

(see photograph on p.33)

NO: 07] REAL TOMATO SOUP

GORDON BROWN
CHANCELLOR OF THE EXCHEQUER

"As a busy MP, I often get back late in the evenings and a quick bowl of soup is just great. If you make big batches of the soup, it can also be frozen in small containers which take no time to defrost in the microwave."

INGREDIENTS

900 g (2 lb) fresh tomatoes

1 medium potato, peeled and cut into small chunks

2 tablespoons olive oil

2 cloves of garlic

1 teaspoon sugar

Salt and pepper, to taste

Chopped parsley or basil for garnish

Fromage frais for garnish (lower on calories than cream)

Oven - 190 °C, 375 F, Gas Mark 5

METHOD

Pre-heat the oven.

Add half the oil to a roasting tin to cover the base of it. Cut each of the tomatoes in half and spread out in the roasting tin. Add the garlic cloves and pour the remaining oil over the tomatoes. Sprinkle with salt and pepper and put in the oven for 30 minutes.

While the tomatoes are roasting, boil the potato in approximately 300 ml (1/2 pint) of water.

Remove the tomatoes from the oven and take off the skins which are now really easy to remove with a fork. Put everything into a food processor - tomatoes, garlic, sugar, potato and potato water and blend it all until it is smooth.

The soup is now ready and just needs to be heated up in a saucepan. A drop of fromage frais and a sprinkling of chopped parsley or basil adds to the flavour and makes it look more attractive to serve to guests.

This soup is great as a starter, but also makes a great meal with toasted cheese and bacon sandwiches or a salad.

SERVES 4

NO: 08] KIPPER & TOMATO SOUP

DAVID & CAROLE HAWKINS
VICAR OF ST. GEORGE'S CHURCH, LEEDS

INGREDIENTS

2 kipper fillets
400 g (14 oz) tin tomatoes
2 tablespoons plain flour
1 small garlic clove
570 ml (1 pint) milk
275 ml (10 fl oz) water
150 ml (5 fl oz) single cream or yoghurt
Salt and pepper, to taste
50 g (2 oz) butter
A dash of lemon juice or sherry

METHOD

Remove most of the skin and bones from the fillets and cut into pieces. Melt the butter in a large saucepan, and add the fillets, tomatoes, garlic and flour. Gradually add the milk and the water. Add salt and pepper to taste. Simmer gently for 20 minutes.

Cool a little and blend in a food processor. Put through a large sieve or small colander to remove any remaining bones. Add cream or yoghurt and re-heat before serving. Add lemon juice or sherry as a final touch.

SERVES 8

In England, more than 103,340 households are currently accepted as homeless and more than 50,000 children are living in temporary accommodation. These statistics on homelessness do not include single homeless people.

NO: 09] CULLEN SKINK

RICHARD WILSON
ACTOR

INGREDIENTS

900 g (2 lb) smoked haddock

1 large onion, chopped

850 ml (1¹/₂ pints) milk

225 g (8 oz) potatoes (or more if you want a thicker soup)

50 g (2 oz) butter, cut into small pieces

Salt and pepper, to taste

A little single cream to serve

METHOD

Boil the potatoes and mash them. Poach the haddock and the onion in a little water. When tender, remove the skin and bones from the fish and flake it. Return the fish to the pan, add the milk and bring to the boil. Add the mashed potato and stir to a creamy consistency. Add the butter, season to taste and add the cream before serving.

SERVES 8

(alternatively as a main course this will serve 4)

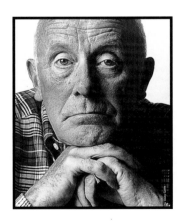

NO: 10] SPECIAL PRAWN COCKTAIL

CILLA BLACK
TV PRESENTER AND ENTERTAINER

INGREDIENTS

225 g (8 oz) fresh prawns

1/2 small melon

8 slices cucumber

4 lettuce leaves

1 lemon

4 tablespoons Hellman's mayonnaise

2 tablespoons tomato ketchup

A dash of Worcestershire sauce or white wine

Garlic, optional

METHOD

To make the sauce, mix the mayonnaise with enough tomato ketchup to give it a pale pink colour. Mix in a dash of Worcestershire sauce and garlic, if desired, to taste. For a very special taste substitute dry white wine for the Worcestershire sauce.

Arrange the prawns in individual dishes on a bed of lettuce and cucumber and top with the sauce. Cover with cling film and place in the refrigerator for 1 hour before serving.

Make melon balls with a butter scoop, or cut into 10 cm (1/2 inch) squares and add to the prawns 15 minutes before serving. Return to the refrigerator.

Serve with lemon cut into wedges. Alternatively, use celery pieces instead of melon.

SERVES 4

NO: 11] WINTER SALAD STARTER

CATHERINE LEWIS

AUTHOR OF 'GOOD FOOD BEFORE BIRTH', UNWIN PAPERBACK 1984

"The French idea of raw vegetables (crudités) as a starter is a good one. Raw food stimulates the right things for digesting food well and getting full food value from the rest of the meal."

INGREDIENTS

2-3 sticks of celery, chopped

4 slices cucumber, 1 cm thick, then diced

1 red apple, chopped into small pieces and tossed in the juice of half a lemon

A handful of walnut halves or pieces

DRESSING

2 tablespoons mayonnaise

2 tablespoons yoghurt

Up to half a teaspoon of French mustard

A squeeze of lemon juice (more if needed to get a light dressing)

METHOD

Prepare the fruit and vegetables. Blend the dressing in a small bowl. Pour over the chopped mixture. Stir to cover the apple and vegetables and top with chopped chives, if available.

SERVES 8

NO: 12] SALMON MOULD

SUE MACGREGOR

PRESENTER OF BBC RADIO 4'S 'TODAY' PROGRAMME

"A summer picnic or lunch recipe from the USA."

INGREDIENTS

125 g ($4^{1}/_{2}$ oz) cooked rice

1 large tin salmon chunks, flaked

100 g (4 oz) good mayonnaise

125 ml (4 fl oz) milk

A dash of lemon juice

1 level dessertspoon gelatine

2 tablespoons water

2 eggs, hard-boiled and sliced

Sliced tomato and cress for decoration

METHOD

Soak the gelatine in the water and dissolve over a gentle heat. Mix with the mayonnaise. Fold in the milk, rice, salmon and lemon juice.

Line the bottom of the mould (preferably ring mould) with sliced eggs, and tomatoes if desired. Add the mixture, cover with foil and leave in the refrigerator to set for at least 2 hours.

Ease gently out of the mould. Decorate with cress, a few shrimps, or a little cream and tomato purée.

SERVES 6-8 OR MORE

(see photograph on p.36)

NO: 13] MELON, GRAPE AND GINGER ORANGE COCKTAIL

ROSEMARY ALFORD
SUPPORTER OF ST. GEORGE'S CRYPT, LEEDS

"A quick and easy starter, which can be prepared well in advance."

INGREDIENTS

1 honeydew melon
200 g (7 oz) seedless grapes
200 ml (7 fl oz) fresh orange juice
Finely grated rind of one orange
50 g (2 oz) caster sugar
1 teaspoon grated fresh root ginger (can be stored in a freezer - easily grated from frozen)

METHOD

Cut the melon in half and remove the seeds. Using a melon-baller, scoop out the flesh into balls and place in a bowl. Wash and halve the grapes and mix with the melon balls. Transfer to 6 individual dishes.

Put the orange juice, grated orange rind, sugar and grated ginger into a saucepan. Place over a low heat and stir until the sugar is dissolved. Cool. Pour over the fruit and serve chilled.

Note : multiple quantities of the juice can be made and kept in rigid containers in the freezer until needed.

SERVES 6

(see photograph on p.37)

NO: 14] BABA GHANOUSH

LESLEY DAWSON

MISSION PARTNER OF ST. GEORGE'S CHURCH, LEEDS, WORKING IN BETHLEHEM

"This recipe is originally from Turkey, but is now eaten all over the Middle East. I like it for two reasons: it is quick and easy to make and delicious to eat. The name of the dish means literally 'Sensitive Father', so this dish would be something that fathers could make to demonstrate their sensitivity!"

INGREDIENTS

1 large aubergine

Juice of 2 lemons

60 g (2 ½ oz) plain yoghurt

A little olive oil

2 garlic cloves, crushed

3 tablespoons tahini

Salt, to taste

Pitta bread to serve

METHOD

Roast the whole aubergine under a grill, turning it a few times until the skin is black and the aubergine feels soft. Peel the skin off and scoop out the inside of the aubergine. Squash the pulp with a fork and add the yoghurt.

Mix together the lemon juice and tahini to make a paste and add the crushed garlic. Mix all these ingredients thoroughly with the aubergine, yoghurt and salt.

Swirl the olive oil on top and serve with hot pitta bread.

To bring out the full flavour, eat with a glass of arak or dry white wine!

SERVES 4

A FACT HOMELESSNESS AND POOR HOUSING CONDITIONS COST THE HEALTH SERVICE APPROXIMATELY £2 BILLION PER YEAR.

NO: 15] CHAWANMUSHI - *japanese steamed egg starter*

HATSUKO NAKAMURA & HEATHER NELSON
STUDENT & MISSION PARTNER OF ST GEORGE'S CHURCH, LEEDS, WORKING IN JAPAN

"This is served as a side dish with the main meal on special occasions in Japan, but I like it as a change from scrambled eggs. It's nice with toast!"

INGREDIENTS

3 eggs
1/2 teaspoon salt
1 1/2 teaspoons soy sauce
1 teaspoon sherry or 1/2 teaspoon sugar
6 small shrimps or prawns
6 mushrooms, chopped small
40 g (1 1/2 oz) frozen runner beans, defrosted and sliced small
100 g (4 oz) chicken, chopped small and marinated in soy sauce for 5 minutes
500 ml (17 fl oz) cold chicken stock (made to half the normal strength) or fish stock, if available

METHOD

Beat the eggs lightly and then mix them with the cold chicken stock, salt, soy sauce and sherry or sugar. Divide the shrimps or prawns, chopped chicken, mushrooms and beans equally into 6 mugs. Pour the egg and stock mixture into the mugs and remove any air bubbles which appear on the surface with a spoon.

Put the mugs into a steaming pan and cover the tops with aluminium foil. Steam for 20-30 minutes over a low heat.

Before removing from the heat, check that the egg mixture is set by inserting a cocktail stick. Remove from the heat and leave to stand for 5 minutes before serving.

SERVES 6

MAIN COURSES

NO: 16] ITALIAN PASTA

JONATHAN EDWARDS

MEN'S TRIPLE JUMP WORLD RECORD HOLDER 1995 & PATRON OF THE 'MORE THAN A ROOF' APPEAL

INGREDIENTS

275 g (10 oz) spaghetti or pasta shapes

225 g (8 oz) bacon

400 g (14 oz) tin chopped tomatoes

175 g (6 oz) mushrooms

Herbs of your own choice, to taste

Salt and pepper, to taste

175 g (6 oz) cheddar cheese, grated

570 ml (1 pint) milk

2 teaspoons cornflour

Oven - 180 °C, 350 F, Gas Mark 4

METHOD

Cook the pasta in boiling salted water for approximately 12-15 minutes or until tender.

Meanwhile, chop the bacon and mushrooms and dry fry. Add the chopped tomatoes and herbs and simmer until the bacon and mushrooms are tender.

Pour almost all the milk into a pan and bring to the boil. Mix the remainder of the milk with the cornflour. When the milk boils, thicken with the cornflour mix and remove from the heat. Add the grated cheese, reserving some to sprinkle on top (see later). Add salt and pepper to taste and stir thoroughly.

Now mix the drained pasta with the bacon mix and the cheese sauce in an ovenproof dish. (Place the dish on a baking tray in case the sauce boils over.) Sprinkle the top with the remaining grated cheese and bake in a pre-heated oven until piping hot, the top is crispy and all the other dishes are washed!

SERVES 2-3

NO: 17] TAGLIATELLE

MICHAEL BUERK
BBC TV NEWSREADER & PRESENTER

INGREDIENTS

350-400 g (12-14 oz) pasta (preferably tagliatelle verdi)
450 g (1 lb) bacon, chopped
4 eggs
Salt and ground black pepper, to taste
2-3 garlic cloves, crushed
425 ml ($^{3}/_{4}$ pint) milk

METHOD

Fry the bacon, and add the garlic to the pan. Beat the eggs and add the milk, salt and pepper.

Meanwhile place the pasta in a large pan of boiling salted water and cook until "al dente", or follow the instructions on the packet.

Add the eggs and milk to the bacon and heat slowly. Be careful not to overheat or the eggs will scramble. When it begins to thicken, add the sauce to the cooked drained pasta. Stir through. The heat of the pasta will finish off cooking the sauce. Serve with Parmesan cheese and a green side salad.

SERVES 4, INCLUDING 2 TEENAGE BOYS!

NO: 18] SPAGHETTI CARBONARA

ANNA FORD

BBC TV NEWSREADER

"This was my mother's recipe. She was a very good cook and a very good mother."

INGREDIENTS

8 rashers smoked bacon

2 tablespoons olive oil

½ wine glass white wine

1 egg (optional)

225 g (8 oz) spaghetti

2 garlic cloves

1 tablespoon butter

110 g (4 oz) cheese, grated

3 tablespoons single cream

METHOD

Place the spaghetti in a pan of boiling salted water and cook for about 7 minutes until "al dente" (still some bite in it), or as indicated on the packet. My children like to throw a piece of the spaghetti at the kitchen wall. If it sticks, it's cooked!

Whilst the pasta is cooking, melt the butter and the oil in a frying pan. Peel and crush the garlic cloves and add to the butter and oil. Cut up the bacon with scissors into roughly 2 ½ cm (1 inch) pieces. Fry in the oil and butter until crisp and brown. Remove from the heat. Carefully add the wine which will clean up all the juices. Sizzle to burn off some of the liquid.

Warm a serving dish in the oven. Add the cream and grated cheese (and uncooked egg - optional) to the warm dish and mix. Strain the spaghetti. Add to the dish and toss. Place the bacon and juices on top and toss.

Serve with a crisp green salad.

SERVES 4

NO: 19] SEAFOOD TAGLIATELLE

ROBSON GREEN
ACTOR & SINGER

INGREDIENTS

450 g (1 lb) fresh tagliatelle

450 g (1 lb) cod

2 tablespoons vegetable oil

1 medium onion

425 ml (¾ pint) milk

4 tablespoons dry white wine

570 ml (1 pint) prawns

450 g (1 lb) salmon

2 garlic cloves

Cornflour to thicken

110 g (4 oz) cheddar or however much you like

METHOD

Place the fresh tagliatelle in a pan of salted water and cook for 3-4 minutes. Meanwhile sauté the garlic and the onion in the oil and wine for about 2 minutes in a large pan. Add the cornflour to make a roux, then pour in the milk and simmer until it thickens. Add the seafood and cook for 2 minutes on a low heat.

Drain the pasta, add the seafood and enjoy.

SERVES 8

NO: 20] SALMON PASTA

GLENN HODDLE

ENGLAND FOOTBALL TEAM COACH & PATRON OF THE 'MORE THAN A ROOF' APPEAL

INGREDIENTS

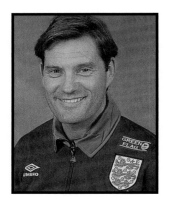

285 g (10 oz) tagliatelle or other pasta

225 g (½ lb) fresh salmon cut into 5 cm (2 inch) pieces

275 ml (10 fl oz) single or whipping cream

85 g (3½ oz) Parmesan cheese, grated

Salt and black pepper, to taste

2 dessertspoons fresh chopped parsley

Lemon slices to garnish

METHOD

Cook the pasta until "al dente" in boiling water.

Meanwhile, steam the salmon for approximately 5 minutes until cooked. Heat the cream gently, then add the Parmesan, salt and pepper and parsley. Add a little milk if the sauce is too thick. Add the salmon and heat through.

Pour the salmon and sauce over the tagliatelle. Garnish with some parsley and lemon slices.

SERVES 4

see recipe on p.17

NO: 21] PAELLA

GARY LINEKER
PRESENTER OF FOOTBALL PROGRAMMES ON BBC TV. FORMER CAPTAIN (1990-1992)
& MEMBER OF THE ENGLAND FOOTBALL TEAM, WITH 80 APPEARANCES BETWEEN 1984 & 1992

This is a dish that Gary enjoyed whilst playing for Barcelona.

INGREDIENTS

2 tablespoons oil	1 onion, peeled and chopped
3 chicken joints, halved	225 g (8 oz) squid rings (optional)
450 g (1 lb) rice	½ teaspoon powdered saffron
1 teaspoon paprika	2 tablespoons tomato purée
1 tablespoon fresh chopped parsley	850 ml (1 ½ pints) chicken stock
Juice of half a lemon	450 g (1 lb) mussels, frozen on the half shell and defrosted
110 g (4 oz) cockles, frozen and shelled	110 g (4 oz) whole prawns

METHOD

Heat the oil in a large frying pan and cook the onion and garlic until soft. Add the chicken pieces and cook for 5 minutes. Add the squid rings and cook for 2 minutes, turning everything over.

Add the rice and stir. Add the saffron, paprika, tomato purée and parsley, then the stock and lemon juice. Bring to the boil, then turn down to simmer. Add the mussels and cockles and cook for 20 minutes, or until the rice is tender.

Ten minutes before the end of the cooking time, add the prawns.

SERVES 6

A FACT CURRENTLY MORE THAN 200 HOMES ARE REPOSSESSED EVERY DAY.

(see photograph on p.40)

NO: 22] FRIDAY NIGHT SPECIAL

JUDITH JACKSON
ST. GEORGE'S CHURCH, LEEDS

INGREDIENTS

4 fish cakes (home made or bought)

1 onion, grated

1 level tablespoon tomatoe purée

1/2 teaspoon sage

1 tablespoon oil

275g (10oz) tin chopped tomatoes

1/2 teaspoon sugar

4 slices processed cheese

METHOD

Heat the oil in the pan and sauté the onion for 2-3 minutes. Add the tomatoes, tomato purée, sage, sugar and seasoning. Simmer for 10 minutes.

Fry or grill the fish cakes, top with the cheese and grill. Pour the tomato sauce over the fish cakes on a serving dish. Serve with peas or green salad and French bread.

SERVES 2

NO: 23] TROUT WITH ALMONDS

PRUNELLA SCALES
ACTRESS

"This is the first meal I ever cooked for my husband Timothy and we have it again sometimes in a spirit of outrageously sentimental gastronomic nostalgia."

INGREDIENTS

2 whole fresh trout

1/4 Ib flaked almonds

Butter

Lemon wedges

METHOD

Gut trout if not already done.

Make three deep incisions on both sides of each fish and place under hot grill with plenty of butter. Cook until really crisp on each side - meanwhile, fry the almond flakes lightly in butter until golden.

Serve with the lemon wedges and any favourite vegetables.

SERVES 2

see recipe on p.23

see recipe on p.24

NO: 24] UN PIOT ET DES PAIS AU FOU (JERSEY BEANS)

JUDITH JACKSON
ST. GEORGE'S CHURCH, LEEDS

*"Every Jersey family has its own recipe of this very old dish.
This one comes from the parish of Grouville. Traditionally it was
cooked in a baker's oven with a pig's trotter and eaten for supper
or breakfast, or cooled and cut like a cake for food for the farmers."*

INGREDIENTS

450 g (1 lb) mixed beans e.g. large and small haricots, red and brown kidney beans, butter beans etc.

Oil for cooking

225 g (8 oz) belly pork

1 large onion

Black treacle, to taste

1 small tin (215 g) baked beans

Salt, pepper, bay leaf, thyme, to taste

METHOD

Soak the beans overnight.

Chop the onion and cook slowly in a heavy saucepan until soft and brown. Cube the pork and place in another pan and brown in the oil. Add the drained beans to the onion, then the pork and pan juices. Cover with water or stock. Bring to the boil and skim off the residue. Add the baked beans and treacle to taste, plus herbs, salt and pepper. Cover and cook on a very low heat for 4-5 hours, topping up with water as necessary.

Serve in soup bowls with bread and butter.

SERVES 6

NO: 25] TANGY PORK AND RICE

VERONICA DORE

USER OF THE FAMILY CENTRE OF ST. GEORGE'S CRYPT, LEEDS

INGREDIENTS

4 pork chops

1/2 teaspoon ground cinnamon

1/2 teaspoon ground coriander

1 litre (2 pints) light stock

2 oranges

1 tablespoon plain flour

3 tablespoons sunflower oil

2 teaspoons turmeric powder

450 g (1 lb) long grain rice

300 ml (1/2 pint) stock

1 large onion, chopped

Salt and pepper

METHOD

Brush the chops with half of the oil and season with salt, pepper and cinnamon. Grill on both sides until cooked.

Bring 2 pints of the light stock to the boil, add the rice and turmeric, and cook according to the instructions on the packet.

Peel the zest from one of the oranges and cut into thin strips. Blanch in boiling water for 1 minute, drain and place to one side. Squeeze the juice from the peeled orange. Slice the other orange for garnish. Fry the onion in the remaining oil until tender, stir in the flour and coriander and cook for 1 minute. Add the remaining stock and squeezed orange juice and bring to the boil, stirring constantly. Simmer for 4 minutes. Add the blanched zest and stir well.

To serve, place the chops on a bed of rice and pour the sauce over. Serve any remaining sauce in a side dish with the orange garnish.

SERVES 4

see recipe on p.34

see recipe on p.42

NO: 26] JO MANAZATTI

MICHAEL FISH
BBC WEATHERMAN

"One of my wife's best concoctions."

INGREDIENTS

900 g (2 lb) lean pork fillet, cut into small pieces

1 large jar tomato purée and 2 cups of water

2 green peppers, sliced

Salt, pepper and cayenne

1 packet small pasta shells (conchiglie)

8 onions, sliced

350 g (12 oz) mushrooms, sliced

450 g (1 lb) strong cheddar cheese, cubed

25 g (1 oz) margarine

Cheese to grate on top

Oven - 180 °C, 350 F, Gas Mark 4

METHOD

Melt the margarine in a large frying pan, brown the onions and pork and put into a large mixing bowl. Add all the other ingredients, except the pasta.

Cook the pasta as indicated on the packet, strain well and add to the mixture.

Put into a large ovenproof casserole dish, grate some cheese on top and put the lid on.

Bake in a pre-heated oven for 1 hour.

This is delicious served with a tossed green salad and garlic bread.

SERVES 10

(see photograph on p.41)

NO: 27] SAUSAGE & CABBAGE CASSEROLE

EMMA THOMPSON
OSCAR-WINNING ACTRESS

"It fills the place with a heavenly smell, and whatever goes on between those sausages and the cabbage produces the best of tastes."

INGREDIENTS

8 sausages - French, Italian, or any good spicy sausage
1 Savoy cabbage
A little butter
Salt and pepper, to taste

Oven - 150 °C, 300 F, Gas Mark 2

METHOD

Cut across the cabbage into approximately 1 inch circles. Parboil the cabbage.

Butter a large casserole with a tight fitting lid.

Place in a layer of cabbage, with a little salt and pepper and butter, followed by a layer of sausage-meat. Continue until full, finishing with cabbage. You can use the big, strong green leaves to cover it up with.

Cook in the oven for 2½-3 hours.

Serve with baked potatoes.

SERVES 4

Dijon Originale

see recipe on p.55

see recipe on p.58

NO: 28] BACON RISOTTO

JOHN MAJOR
PRIME MINISTER OF GREAT BRITAIN & NORTHERN IRELAND, 1990-1997

INGREDIENTS

50 g (2 oz) butter
1 large onion, chopped
125 g (4¹/₂ oz) mushrooms, sliced
175 g (6 oz) long grain rice
600-900 ml (1-1¹/₂ pints) stock
175 g (6 oz) cooked bacon/ham
125 g (4¹/₂ oz) cooked peas
200 g (7 oz) tin sweetcorn with peppers
Salt and pepper, to taste
Sultanas, optional

METHOD

Melt the butter in a large frying pan, add the onion and sauté for 5 minutes. Add the mushrooms, stir and cook for a few seconds. Stir in the rice and 600 ml (1 pint) of stock. Cover and simmer for 20-25 minutes until the rice is cooked. If necessary, add extra stock.

Cube the bacon and add to the rice with the remaining ingredients. Season with pepper. Cook for a further 5 minutes to heat through. Add salt to taste. A few sultanas may also be added, if liked.

SERVES 4

STATISTIC 18% OF RENTED PRIVATE SECTOR HOUSING IS UNFIT FOR HUMAN HABITATION; 1.8% LACK ONE OR MORE BASIC AMENITIES.

NO: 29] QUICK FRIED RICE

CAROL VORDERMAN
TV PRESENTER

"This recipe was given to my mother when she lived in Holland and it continues to be the favourite dish of all the Vordermans."

INGREDIENTS

225 g (8 oz) 'quick cook' or 'easy cook' rice

150 g (6 oz) bacon (bacon bits are ideal)

2 eggs

2-3 tablespoons vegetable oil

1 large onion (or 2 medium-sized)

1 heaped teaspoon Marmite (or similar savoury spread)

Soy sauce, optional

METHOD

Boil the rice according to the instructions on the packet. Strain the rice through a colander and rinse it with very hot water to separate the grains. Leave the rice in the colander until required.

Trim and cut the bacon into little pieces. Peel and slice the onion. Beat the eggs. Dissolve the Marmite in a cupful of boiling water and stir well.

Heat the oil in a very large frying pan and add the bacon pieces. Set the pieces aside. Next, lightly sauté the sliced onion in the pan and return the bacon bits. Mix the bacon and onions together and then slowly pour the beaten eggs over the mixture. Let the eggs cook very slowly, constantly stirring the mixture.

Start adding the cooked rice to the mixture and keep stirring until all the oil has been absorbed. At this point add the cupful of Marmite mixture to the pan, bring the mixture back to the boil and then simmer. Keep adding the remainder of the rice to the mixture, stirring well. Mix it all up thoroughly. If the mixture is a little too wet just let it simmer gently until the excess moisture has evaporated.

Serve piping hot with soy sauce (if liked).

With this recipe you can use up all sorts of leftovers or add other ingredients (e.g. mushrooms, mixed herbs etc.) to your taste.

SMAKELIJK ETEN!

SERVES 2-4

see recipe on p.59

NO: 30] AMERICAN BRUNCH

COURTNEY LEWIS
FINALIST OF BBC TV JUNIOR MASTERCHEF 1997

"For me, this meal conjures up memories of holidays in California, freedom from school, cloudless skies and unstructured days."

INGREDIENTS

8 rashers maple cured bacon (this is available from all good supermarkets, and gives the meal a real American taste!)
2 tablespoons olive oil

4 eggs

Maple syrup (this is the predominant flavour, so make sure you don't buy an imitation brand.

Although the real type may be more expensive, it's worth the extra!)

PANCAKES
110 g (4 oz) self-raising flour

200 ml (7 fl oz) milk

3 tablespoons caster sugar

3 eggs

A knob of butter, for frying

HASHBROWNS
500 g (1 lb 2 oz) parboiled potatoes, peeled and cooked whole   1 large onion

Freshly milled salt and pepper, to taste   50 g (2 oz) butter

METHOD

First make the pancakes (should make 16). Mix the ingredients (not butter) together thoroughly. There should be absolutely no lumps, and the mixture should not be too runny, or too thick. Turn on a ring at a medium heat. Melt the butter in a frying pan, making sure the butter doesn't burn. Drop in 2 tablespoons of batter. Keep the pancake quite thick and no more then 15 cm (6 inch) in diameter. When bubbles begin to appear on the surface, turn it over. Each side should take approximately 2 minutes. Keep the pancakes in a warm oven (70 °C, 160 F) until they are all ready.

Next, make the hashbrowns. Grate the potatoes and onions quite thickly, and mix together with plenty of salt and pepper. Press into 8 cakes, using a 10 cm (4 inch) scone cutter. For each hashbrown, melt a little butter in a non-stick pan. Fry on each side for about 5 minutes, until brown and crisp.

Finally, cook the bacon and egg. Fry the bacon in a tablespoon of olive oil until crisp. Scrape any little bits of bacon or hashbrown out of the pan. Add a final tablespoon of olive oil, and make everyone a fried egg, sunny side up.

To serve, put the stack of four pancakes in the middle of the plate, and pour maple syrup over it. Pop the egg on top. Add a hashbrown on each side of the plate, topped with bacon. It's delicious, but definitely not one for the calorie counters!

SERVES 4

NO: 31] CALIFORNIAN BAKED BEANS

BEL MOONEY
NOVELIST, CHILDREN'S AUTHOR & BROADCASTER

"When I was 17, I went on an Easter CND March in London, and my friend Helen and I volunteered for a silent vigil outside the Houses of Parliament. It was bitterly cold and when we had done our shift we ran to the tube, frozen. When we reached the place we were staying, our American hostess, a friend of Helen's parents, had the following supper dish waiting for us and it tasted better than anything I had ever eaten in my life. I asked for the recipe and it was the first dish I learned to cook."

INGREDIENTS

1 mug dried haricot beans, soaked overnight

1 tin chopped tomatoes, drained

450g (1 lb) best mince

Salt and pepper, to taste

1 large Spanish onion, thinly sliced

About 6 rashers streaky bacon

3/4 tablespoon brown sugar (do not leave out)

Oven - 180 °C, 350 F, Gas Mark 4

METHOD

Cook the beans for about 1 hour, until tender, adding salt to taste in the last 30 minutes of cooking time. Drain and put on one side. In a large frying pan, brown the meat, and then add the tomatoes. Season and cook for 10 minutes. Add the beans and cook for another 5 minutes.

On the bottom of a casserole dish put half the sliced onions, then half the mixture from the pan. Sprinkle with half of the sugar, then add the rest of the onions. Then add the rest of the bean mixture. On the top, lay the strips of bacon to cover, and top the bacon with the rest of the sugar. Cook in the oven for 1 hour, and serve with jacket potatoes, or chunks of good crusty bread.

SERVES 6

NO: 32] KILLER CHILLI

LENNY HENRY
COMEDIAN

INGREDIENTS

450 g (1 lb) minced beef

2 big onions

1 tin Italian tomatoes

110g (4 oz) butter

A pinch of oregano

A pinch of cloves

Glass of red wine

110g (4 oz) mushrooms, chopped

Chilli powder - mild or not-
-depending on whether your tongue is made of leather!

110 g (4 oz) butter

2 green peppers

1 tin kidney beans

1 tablespoon tomato purée

A pinch of mixed spices

A dash of tabasco

2 beef Oxo cubes

A lucky rabbit's foot !

METHOD

Place the rabbit's foot around your neck. (You're going to need all the luck you can get because I certainly don't know what I'm doing.)

Chop the onions and the green peppers and sauté in the butter until they are fairly translucent (that means see-through, thicky). Add the meat to the pan and brown. Add the tomatoes and stir for 2 minutes until it is bubbling noisily. Add the tomato purée and stir until the sauce thickens. Add all the spices, herbs and chopped mushrooms and stir for 2 minutes. Add the kidney beans and mix in. Add a dash of tabasco and crumble in the Oxo cubes and the wine and stir again.

Cover and simmer over a low heat for about 1 hour, stirring occasionally. After this time it should be a lovely dark brown colour and quite thick. If there is a layer of fat on the top, remove with a spoon.

Yum Yum in my Tum! Serve with rice or pitta bread.

SERVES 4

NO: 33] BOBOTIE

RICHARD BRANSON
BUSINESSMAN & ENTREPRENEUR

INGREDIENTS

1 tablespoon oil

450 g (1 lb) lean mince

1 apple, peeled and chopped

1 tablespoon mango chutney

1 tablespoon lemon juice

1 large onion, finely chopped

50 g (2 oz) flaked almonds

1 tablespoon curry powder

40 g (1½ oz) sultanas

150 ml (5 fl oz) beef stock or red wine

TOPPING

2 free range eggs

20 g (¾ oz) butter

Salt and pepper, to taste

20 g (¾ oz) flour

300 ml (½ pint) milk

Oven - 180 °C, 350 F, Gas Mark 4

METHOD

Pre-heat the oven.

Sauté the onion in the oil until transparent. Add the mince and brown. Add the chopped apple, curry powder, almonds and sultanas. Cook for about 5 minutes, then add the chutney, stock/wine and lemon juice. Add the salt and pepper and additional curry powder to taste. Transfer to a 1½ litre (2½ pint) pie dish and bake in the oven for 15 minutes.

Meanwhile, make the topping. Melt the butter, add the flour and stir in the milk, being careful not to let the sauce go lumpy. When the sauce has thickened, take off the heat and allow to cool slightly before adding the eggs. Stir in the eggs and add salt and pepper.

Remove the main dish from the oven (it should have formed a slight crust) and pour the sauce over it. Return it to the oven and bake for about 40 minutes until the top is slightly browned.

Serve with rice and salad.

SERVES 4

NO: 34] HUMITA PIE

JOYCE ILLINGWORTH

MISSION PARTNER OF ST. GEORGE'S CHURCH, LEEDS, WORKING IN ARGENTINA

INGREDIENTS

TOPPING

2 tins (400 g; 14 oz) whole grain corn (or frozen corn)

75 g (3 oz) finely chopped red or green (or both)

pepper to give colour and flavour

Ground pepper and salt, to taste

1 small onion, grated (or very finely chopped)

A little oil

1 egg, beaten

110 g (4 oz) (or more if liked)

Parmesan cheese or cheddar cheese

BASE

250g (9 oz) minced meat

A small tin plum tomatoes, chopped with juice

Ground pepper, salt, oregano, a pinch of ground cumin

1 small onion

1 garlic clove, crushed

1 tablespoon oil

Oven - 180 °C, 350 F, Gas Mark 4

METHOD

To make the base, lightly sauté the onion. Add the meat and stir until it is coated with oil. Add the tomatoes and cook gently for 10 minutes until the meat is cooked. Add the seasoning and put in the bottom of a greased ovenproof dish.

To make the topping, process the corn into a granular consistency. Add the cheese, chopped onion, chopped peppers and seasoning. Mix well. Add a little beaten egg or oil if it looks dry. Spread on top of the meat and cook for 30 minutes. Alternatively the cheese can be sprinkled on top, halfway through cooking, allowing it to brown slightly.

SERVES 4

NO: 35] FORSYTH'S STEAK DIJON

BRUCE FORSYTH
TV PRESENTER & PERSONALITY

As served at the 'Wig and Pen Club' in London.

INGREDIENTS

1 sirloin steak

English mustard to taste

Demerara sugar to taste

METHOD

Grill both sides of the steak to your liking. On one side, spread a generous amount of mustard.

Sprinkle demerara sugar on top of the mustard, again be generous. Put under a very hot grill until the sugar starts to bubble and caramelises.

Serve with new potatoes and a salad or vegetables of your own choice.

SERVES 1

ARE YOU AWARE? THE NUMBER OF EMPTY HOUSES IN ENGLAND LAST YEAR WAS 767,000; SEVEN TIMES THE NUMBER OF HOMELESS HOUSEHOLDS.

NO: 36] PEPPER STEAK

ANTHONY WORRALL THOMPSON
RESTAURATEUR & TV CHEF

"This is a forgotten 60's dish that should be remembered as it is delicious. It is one of the first restaurant dishes I learnt to cook. I hope you enjoy this dish as much as I do."

INGREDIENTS

1 tablespoon crushed white peppercorns	1 tablespoon crushed black peppercorns
450 g (1 lb) rump or sirloin steak in one piece, 40 mm (1½ inch) thick	½ tablespoon good olive oil
50 g (2 oz) unsalted butter	2 shallots, finely diced
2 teaspoons Worcestershire sauce	2 tablespoons brandy
90 ml (3 fl oz) beef stock	½ tablespoon Dijon mustard
3 tablespoons double cream	Salt, to taste

Prepare 2-3 hours in advance

METHOD

Make sure the steak is dry. Press the mixed peppercorns into both sides of the steak by pushing with your hands. If you have time, cover with foil or cling film and leave the pepper flavour to infuse into the steak for 2-3 hours, in the refrigerator.

Pour the oil into a heavy-based frying pan and, over a high heat, seal the steak for 2 minutes on each side. Reduce the heat, add half the butter to the pan, and cook the steak for 5-10 minutes depending on how rare you like your steak. Remove the steak to a warm place and set aside.

Pour away most of the fat, add the remaining butter with the shallots and over a medium heat sauté the shallots until soft but not brown. Pour in the Worcestershire sauce and stock and cook rapidly, scraping the bottom of the pan Fold in the mustard and cream and season to taste.

Slice the steak on the diagonal and add to the sauce. Stir to combine the meat juices with the pepper sauce and warm the meat through, but do not re-boil. Heat the brandy in a ladle over a flame until it ignites and pour over the steak. Serve with chips or new potatoes and a watercress salad.

SERVES 2

(see photograph on p.44)

NO: 37] BEEF WELLINGTON

DAVID GOWER
TV SPORTS COMMENTATOR & FORMER CAPTAIN OF THE ENGLAND CRICKET TEAM

INGREDIENTS

1.4 kg (3 lb) beef fillet

225 g (8 oz) mushrooms, finely chopped

1 egg, beaten

1 tablespoon oil

Salt and pepper, to taste

110 g (4 oz) paté

450 g (1 lb) puff pastry, or shortcrust

(see section on handy basics)

Oven - 230 °C, 450 F, Gas Mark 8

METHOD

Preheat the oven. Rub the beef with salt, pepper and the oil. Roast on a rack for 40 minutes. Remove and leave to cool.

When cool, cover the top and sides with the paté and chopped mushrooms.

Roll out the pastry to 5 mm (¼ inch) thickness - large enough to envelope the meat. Put the fillet top side down on the pastry, and enclose into a parcel sealing the ends. Turn the meat seam down and decorate with the spare pastry (if you can be bothered!). Glaze with the beaten egg.

Bake for a further 40 minutes or so, till the pastry is golden brown and puffed up.

This tastes even better if served with a red wine sauce.

SERVES 6-8

(see photograph on p.54

NO: 38] MOROCCAN LAMB TAGINE

JENNIE BOND
BBC TV NEWS REPORTER & ROYAL COURT CORRESPONDENT

"I like it because it was one of my husband's first recipes when he joined a cookery class this year. Wednesdays have become days of culinary feasts as he arrives home with his latest creations - and this was one of the best."

INGREDIENTS

2 tablespoons oil

700 g (1½ lb) cubed lamb

1 teaspoon ground cumin

A large pinch of saffron

1 onion, finely chopped

1 teaspoon ground cinnamon

1 tablespoon sesame seeds

50 g (2 oz) blanched almonds

2 garlic cloves, crushed

275 ml (½ pint) stock

2 tablespoons clear honey

1 teaspoon fresh root ginger

A large bunch of fresh parsley, chopped

½ small lemon, cut into small pieces

Salt and pepper, to taste

METHOD

Heat the oil in a large pan and sauté the ginger, garlic and onion until soft. Add the lamb, saffron and half the parsley. Then pour in the stock to barely cover, and simmer very gently for 1½ hours, stirring occasionally.

Add the cinnamon, cumin and the lemon. Mix well and cook for 15 minutes. Stir in the honey, cover and continue to cook for a further 5 minutes.

Dry fry the sesame seeds. Stir the remaining parsley into the tagine and season to taste, then sprinkle with the sesame seeds and blanched almonds. Serve with boiled rice.

SERVES 6

NO: 39] SMOKED CHICKEN SALAD

LORD JEFFREY ARCHER
POLITICIAN & AUTHOR

"I have chosen this recipe because not only is it very tasty and healthy (as long as you go easy on the mayonnaise) but sadly it is the only thing I can cook!"

INGREDIENTS

SALAD
450 g (1 lb) cooked chicken (or left-over turkey) cut into thin strips

1 bunch spring onions, washed and chopped

110 g (4 oz) bean sprouts, washed and well drained

1 crisp lettuce

50 g (2 oz) button mushrooms, quartered

1/2 cucumber, chopped into chunks

1 avocado, peeled and chopped

Juice of 1/2 lemon

6 quails eggs (hen's eggs could be used), hard-boiled for 5 minutes, shelled and quartered

110 g (4 oz) smoked streaky bacon, fried until crisp, drained and crumbled

Croutons, to garnish

A handful of raisins (optional)

DRESSING
1 small carton low fat yoghurt

50 g (2 oz) blue cheese

2 tablespoons mayonnaise

Salt and pepper

METHOD

Wash and dry the lettuce carefully, tear into shreds and place in a salad bowl. Add all the other ingredients, except the croutons, and squeeze the lemon juice over to prevent the avocado discolouring.

To make the dressing, whisk all the ingredients together. Pour over the salad and fold in carefully.

SERVES 8 AS A MAIN COURSE
(or 12-15 as an accompaniment)

(see photograph on p.45)

NO: 40] SWEET & SOUR CHICKEN

STEPHEN HENDRY

SIX-TIMES WORLD SNOOKER CHAMPION

INGREDIENTS

4 chicken portions

2 tablespoons dripping or oil

2 tablespoons soy sauce

1 tablespoon wine vinegar

1 onion, peeled and sliced

1 tablespoon plain flour

Freshly boiled rice to serve 4

Salt and freshly ground black pepper, to taste

200 g (7 oz) tin pineapple rings

2 tablespoons tomato ketchup

1 tablespoon soft brown sugar

1 red or green pepper, cored, sliced and peeled

400 g (14 oz) tin tomatoes

Oven - 180 °C, 350 F, Gas Mark 4

METHOD

Season the chicken portions all over with salt and pepper. Heat the oil or dripping in a frying pan, add the chicken and fry until well browned all over. Transfer to a large casserole dish.

Drain the pineapple, keeping the syrup and chop 2 of the rings and sprinkle over the chicken. Reserve the remaining pineapple for the garnish. Make up the syrup to 150 ml (1/4 pint) with water and add the soy sauce, ketchup, vinegar and sugar to the syrup.

Add the onion and red or green pepper to the frying pan and fry in the same fat until tender. Stir in the flour and cook for 1 minute. Add the pineapple syrup mixture and tomatoes and bring to the boil, stirring well. Add salt and pepper to taste and simmer for 2 minutes. Pour over the chicken.

Cover the casserole and cook in a pre-heated oven for about 45 minutes or until the chicken is tender. Serve with freshly boiled rice and garnish each piece of chicken with half a pineapple ring.

SERVES 4

(see photograph on p.48)

NO: 41] CHICKEN PIECES IN BLACK BEAN SAUCE

SIR ALAN AYCKBOURN
PLAYWRIGHT & ARTISTIC DIRECTOR

'I started cooking chinese food about 8 years ago and very much enjoy it. It's also an excellent diet if you want to lose weight!"

INGREDIENTS

450 g (1 lb) chicken wings or chicken pieces, unskinned

1 tablespoon dry sherry or rice wine

1 tablespoon fresh ginger, finely chopped

1½ tablespoons spring onions, finely chopped

150 ml (5 fl oz) chicken stock

1 tablespoon light soy sauce

2 teaspoons oil (preferably ground nut)

1 tablespoon garlic, finely chopped

1½ tablespoons black beans, coarsely chopped

Marinating time - 1 hour

METHOD

If you are using chicken wings, cut them in half at the joint. If you are using chicken pieces, cut them into 5 cm (2 inch) chunks. Mix the soy sauce and sherry (or rice wine) together and pour it over the chicken pieces. Let the chicken marinate for about 1 hour, then drain the chicken and discard the marinade.

Heat the wok or large frying pan. Add the oil and when it is hot add the ginger. Stir-fry it for a few seconds and then add the garlic, spring onions and black beans. A few seconds later add the chicken and stir-fry for 2-5 minutes at a high heat until they are brown. Then add the stock. Bring the mixture to the boil and then reduce the heat.

Simmer for 15 minutes or until the chicken is cooked, adding more water if necessary to stop the mixture becoming too dry. (If you are using chicken breasts, cook for just 5 minutes.) This dish can be cooked ahead of time and re-heated, making sure the chicken is re-heated thoroughly. It is also delicious served cold.

SERVES 4

NO: 42] THAI CHICKEN

JANE WOODHEAD
MEMBER OF THE MUMS' GROUP OF ST. GEORGE'S CHURCH, LEEDS

"Delicious served with rice and salad."

INGREDIENTS

4-6 boneless chicken fillets

275 ml (1/2 pt) boiling water

1-2 teaspoons ground ginger

Grated zest and juice of 1-2 limes

2 tablespoons fresh coriander

A hint of lemon grass

200 g (7 oz) block of creamed coconut

3-4 garlic cloves, peeled and chopped

3 tablespoons light soy sauce

2 level tablespoons caster sugar

3 green chillies, finely chopped

Oven - 180 °C, 350 F, Gas Mark 4

METHOD

Dissolve the coconut in boiling water. Place all the ingredients (except the chicken) into a jug. Pour over the chicken and place in a refrigerator to marinate for 2 hours. Cook in a casserole in a pre-heated oven for 1¼ hours, until tender.

The sauce does separate if the temperature of the oven is too high, but easily remixes.

SERVES 4-6

STATISTIC 48% OF LANDLORDS WILL NOT RENT TO PEOPLE ON HOUSING BENEFIT.
THIS MEANS THAT THE OPTIONS FOR PEOPLE ON LOW-INCOMES ARE SHRINKING ALL THE TIME.

NO: 43] ROSEANNE'S LEMON CHICKEN

BETTY BOOTHROYD

SPEAKER OF THE HOUSE OF COMMONS

"This is one of my favourite recipes as it is fairly quick and easy to cook, tastes delicious and I enjoy it very much."

INGREDIENTS

4 chicken breasts

Grated rind and juice of 2 lemons

1 stick of celery, chopped

Salt and pepper, to taste

Watercress and lemon twists to garnish

1-2 tablespoons olive oil

1 onion, sliced

A few sprigs of thyme

275 ml (½ pint) chicken stock

Marinating time - 3-4 hours

Oven - 190 °C, 375 F, Gas Mark 5

METHOD

Brush the chicken breasts with the olive oil. Place in an ovenproof dish or tin with the lemon rind and juice and leave to marinate for 3-4 hours in a refrigerator.

Make the chicken stock and leave to cool.

Add the onion, celery, thyme, salt, pepper and chicken stock and cook for about 1 hour.

Garnish and serve with rice.

SERVES 4

NO: 44] CHICKEN WITH FORTY CLOVES OF GARLIC

CHERYL BAKER
TV PRESENTER

INGREDIENTS

4 chicken breast fillets (boneless)

6 tablespoons olive oil

Lots of fresh sprigs of rosemary, sage and parsley

1 stick of celery, chopped

Salt and freshly milled black pepper, to taste

4 sprigs thyme

1 bay leaf

40 cloves of garlic, unpeeled

Oven - 190 °C, 375 F, Gas Mark 5

METHOD

Make a pocket in each fillet of chicken, season with salt and pepper and insert a sprig of thyme.
Place the oil in a medium-sized casserole dish (with a lid) and add the remaining herbs, chopped celery and unpeeled cloves of garlic. Lay the chicken on top and roll it over and over so it is coated with the herbs and oil.

Cook in a pre-heated oven for 1½ hours.

Bring the pot to the table so that as you take the lid off, everyone will smell the delicious aroma.

Serve with absolutely anything you like!

SERVES 4

NO: 45] SPICY CHICKEN

ELIZABETH TAYLOR
OSCAR-WINNING ACTRESS

INGREDIENTS

2 teaspoons curry powder

1/2 teaspoon ground ginger

1/2 clove garlic, crushed

1 teaspoon fresh ginger, grated

1 teaspoon cumin

1/2 teaspoon turmeric

1 onion, chopped

1 medium chicken-
-cut into serving pieces and skinned

Marinating time - 2 hours

METHOD

Combine the dry ingredients with the garlic, onion and fresh grated ginger. Coat the chicken with the mixture and refrigerate for 2 hours, preferably longer. Place on a moderately hot barbecue or grill for approximately 30 minutes, or until done, turning once.

SERVES 4

NO: 46] POTAGE YEHUDI MENUHIN

LORD YEHUDI MENUHIN
VIOLINIST & CONDUCTOR

INGREDIENTS

350 g (12 oz) vegetables to include onion, carrot, leek, swede, celeriac, celery and courgette
(keep courgette and leek separate)

1 whole baby chicken

Mixed herbs - parsley, tarragon, chervil, chives, basil

1 bulb garlic

4 egg yolks

300 ml (11 fl oz) extra virgin olive oil

1 litre (1¾ pints) water

General seasonings - salt, pepper, bay leaf

METHOD

Portion the chicken into small joints, place the trimmings and carcass to one side. Prepare and dice the vegetables into ½ cm (¼ inch) pieces. Using the vegetable trimmings, chicken carcass, herb stalks and general seasonings make a chicken stock, with ¾ litre (1¼ pints) of water.

Warm 6 cloves of garlic (do not crush) in half the olive oil to soften and infuse the flavour. Split the remaining olive oil into 2 pans, add 2 split garlic cloves to each and warm. In one pan gently sauté the chicken pieces, cover with the chicken stock and cook gently. Sweat the vegetables in the other pan until soft, adding the leek and courgette at the end. When the chicken is cooked pour the stock onto the vegetables and bring back to the boil slowly. (You may add the rest of the water if required.)

Remove the chicken meat from any skin or bone and place aside. Skim the broth, remove from the heat, add freshly chopped herbs and chicken meat and check the seasoning.

Take 2 egg yolks, add a little broth to make a sabayon. Add the garlic infused in olive oil SLOWLY to make a 'warm mayonnaise'. Add the softened garlic cloves to the soup.

To serve - bring back to the boil, remove from the heat for 30 seconds, fork in the remaining 2 egg yolks and gently stir in the mayonnaise. Sprinkle with chopped fresh herbs.

SERVES 4

© Yehudi Menuhin and Robert Kisby, 1997.

Chef's tip - To portion the chicken, pull the legs away from the body and cut down between the two legs until the legs come away. Carefully cut down to one side of the backbone, pulling the breast away from the carcass until it comes away and repeat on the other side.

NO: 47] CHICKEN & BOUDINS NOIR

JEREMY PAXMAN
BBC TV PRESENTER

INGREDIENTS

1 chicken
2 French black puddings - I feel it is important to get the authentic article (boudins noir) because they are much richer than the English ones and have a higher blood content. This could provide an excuse for a long weekend in Paris!

METHOD

Split the boudins noir, remove the filling and use it to stuff the chicken. Roast the chicken in the usual way for a stuffed chicken. Cook it upside down for at least half the cooking time so that the breast becomes infused with the flavour of the boudin.

NO: 48] CALVADOS PHEASANTS

BARONESS MARGARET THATCHER
PRIME MINISTER OF GREAT BRITAIN & NORTHERN IRELAND, 1979-1990

INGREDIENTS

1 brace pheasants - jointed

40 g (1½ oz) butter

10 shallots, peeled

Herbes De Provence

225 g (8 oz) mushrooms

275 ml (10 fl oz) calvados

275 ml (10 fl oz) stock

350 g (12 oz) streaky bacon

2 garlic cloves, chopped

2 bay leaves

275 ml (10 fl oz) dry white wine

2 tablespoons oil

METHOD

Season the pheasant joints and fry in butter and 1 tablespoon of oil until golden brown. Transfer to a casserole dish. Sauté the shallots in the remaining oil, and remove to a plate. Chop the bacon and fry, remove to the plate.

Add the herbs, bay leaves and garlic to the pheasant, then add the stock, wine and calvados. Bring to a simmer, cover and cook for 45 minutes. Add the mushrooms, bacon and shallots and simmer for a further 45 minutes.

Place the pheasants on a pre-heated dish. Boil the sauce and reduce to thicken. Pour the sauce over the pheasant and serve.

SERVES 4-6

ST. GEORGE'S CRYPT, LEEDS
the night social & emergency centre

Each evening in the Crypt building our staff provide food, friendship, shelter, advice and referrals for accommodation. Last year, our Night Social Centre recorded 24,230 visits involving a greater proportion of young people, women, members of ethnic minority groups and individuals suffering from mental illness. The Friends' Group (made up of users of the Crypt) work together with volunteers and staff members to improve the services and type of support provided through this centre.

During the day the Crypt offers an NHS-clinic for rootless people (once a week), a clothes store and advice centre for homeless men and women.

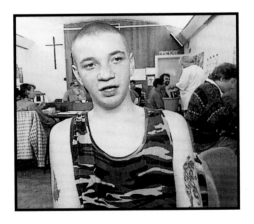

"I sleep on the streets and sleeping on the streets leads to drugs and crime, and crime leads to prison".

We are dedicated to helping young people like this to break out of this vicious cycle and improve their lifestyle.

This young man is now in settled accommodation.

Through our 3 hostels, 24 otherwise homeless men and women are offered short- to medium-term accommodation, encouraging self-help, a more stable lifestyle and assistance to obtain and keep their own accommodation.

VEGETARIAN MEALS
& side dishes

NO: 49] PENNE ARABIATA AL DONATO

SIR ANTHONY HOPKINS
OSCAR-WINNING ACTOR

This recipe is made with monotonous regularity by Donato at Sandrini's Restaurant nearly every time Sir Anthony goes there! Donato said that this dish should never be served with Parmesan cheese as it spoils the flavour. It is a simple, typically Italian dish and its secret is a good tomato sauce made from tinned Italian plum tomatoes or slightly over-ripe fresh ones.

INGREDIENTS

4 tins (225 g; 8 oz) Italian plum tomatoes - roughly chopped

2 garlic cloves, finely chopped

1 teaspoon sugar

2 tablespoons olive oil

1 chilli, or chilli powder, to taste

1 large Spanish onion, finely chopped

Basil, to taste

Salt and pepper, to taste

275 g (10 oz) penne pasta

Chopped parsley to garnish

METHOD

First, make the tomato sauce. Sauté the onions with the garlic and basil in about 1 tablespoon of olive oil in a saucepan on a medium heat until transparent. Add the tomatoes, sugar and salt and pepper. Turn down the heat and simmer to reduce for 30 minutes. Do not cover. Purèe the mixture through a sieve or Moulinex grater - preferably not a liquidiser like a Magimix.

Bring a large saucepan of water to the boil, add the pasta, stir and simmer for 5-10 minutes, depending on the type of pasta. It should be slightly hard ("al dente"). Strain and then transfer to a warmed dish.

Put some olive oil, finely chopped chilli or chilli powder and some chopped parsley in a sturdy frying pan and sauté quickly on a high heat until brown. Now add this to the tomato sauce and pour over the pasta. Garnish with parsley.

Serve with a green salad and ciabatta bread, which can be dipped in balsamic vinegar and extra virgin olive oil on a side plate.

SERVES 4

Sponsored by

MARKS & SPENCER

NO: 50] WALNUT PASTA

JONATHAN DIMBLEBY
BBC TV & RADIO PRESENTER

"This is a recipe that my wife often used to make when she hadn't planned anything and had to rely on the store cupboard, and parsley from the garden. My favourite evenings are when we can sit down together at the kitchen table, with a bottle of good red wine, and eat something as delicious as this. It is best served with a mixed salad and good conversation!"

INGREDIENTS

175 g (6 oz) fine spaghetti

2 fat spring onions, chopped, using much of the green

25 g (1 oz) parsley

25 g (1 oz) cheese e.g emmenthal-
-or a blue cheese if liked, finely diced

2 tablespoons walnut oil

50 g (2 oz) walnuts, chopped

Freshly ground black pepper, to taste

METHOD

Boil the spaghetti in plenty of salted water, and have a warm dish ready. While the spaghetti is cooking, finely chop at least half the parsley, reserving the rest for garnish. Heat the walnut oil in a small pan and gently sauté the spring onions. Add the chopped walnuts and fry to colour.

When the spaghetti is cooked tip it into the dish, and quickly add the mixture from the pan. Throw in the cheese and the parsley and toss it about, not wasting time. Cover and serve immediately with freshly ground black pepper. The cheese should be melting but still retain some shape.

SERVES 2

NO: 51] PASTA WITH TWO CHEESES

PADDY ASHDOWN
MP & LEADER OF THE LIBERAL DEMOCRATS

INGREDIENTS

400 g (14 oz) tin plum tomatoes

1 tablespoon of olive oil (any oil will do)

50 g (2 oz) mature cheddar cheese, grated

110-175 g (4-6 oz) pasta, any sort

1 garlic clove, chopped

2 teaspoons of dried basil or 5 fresh basil leaves

125 g (5 oz) Mozzarella cheese, chopped into cubes

METHOD

Put a large pan of slightly salted water on to boil.

In a heavy-based pan, mash the tomatoes with the back of a wooden spoon, add the oil, basil and garlic, and simmer gently so that the sauce thickens.

When the water boils, add the pasta, following the cooking instructions on the pack.

Now add the two cheeses to the tomato sauce, turning the heat right down. Stir well once, then leave while the pasta finishes cooking. If the sauce starts to stick, turn off the heat and cover with a lid to keep it hot.

Pour the sauce over the pasta and serve.

SERVES 2

NO: 52] MACARONI CHEESE

DESMOND LYNAM
BBC TV SPORTS PRESENTER

"I enjoy this meal because it is simple to make and is quite delicious."

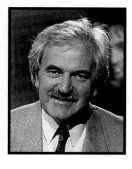

INGREDIENTS

175 g (6 oz) macaroni

4 level tablespoons flour

A pinch of grated nutmeg

175 g (6 oz) mature cheese, grated

Salt and pepper, to taste

40 g ($1^{1}/_{2}$ oz) butter

570 ml (1 pint) milk

$^{1}/_{2}$ teaspoon mustard

2 tablespoons fresh white breadcrumbs (optional)

Oven - 200 °C, 400 F, Gas Mark 6

METHOD

Cook the macaroni for 10 minutes in boiling, salted water.

Melt the butter in a saucepan and stir in the flour and gradually add the milk. Bring to the boil slowly, stirring the sauce until it thickens. Remove from the heat, add the seasoning and about 120g ($4^{1}/_{2}$ oz) of the cheese. Add the macaroni to the sauce, giving it a good stir, then pour into an ovenproof dish and sprinkle with breadcrumbs (if required) and the remaining cheese. Cook in the oven for about 20 minutes or until golden and bubbling.

SERVES 2

"I ACHE ALL OVER FROM SLEEPING ON THE PAVEMENT, BUT I ACHE INSIDE TOO FROM THE LOOKS I GET FROM PEOPLE PASSING BY. THEY THINK I DON'T CARE; THEY THINK I'M NOT HUMAN." **- BILLY, A YOUNG HOMELESS PERSON.**

NO: 53] WAIKIKI DELIGHT
vegetarian croquettes in a sweet and sour sauce served over rice

JUDITH SHALKOWSKI
MEMBER OF THE MUMS' GROUP OF ST. GEORGE'S CHURCH, LEEDS

"Easily confused as meat by non-vegetarians."

INGREDIENTS

CROQUETTES

4 eggs, separated

1 medium onion, finely chopped

2 tablespoons parsley, chopped

160 g (5 oz) Edam cheese (low fat), grated

180 g (6 oz) rolled oats (not instant)

35 g (1½ oz) rolled oats (ground to flour
consistency for coating croquettes)

2 tablespoons oil for frying

SAUCE

2 tablespoons cornflour

6 tablespoons honey or golden syrup

450 g (16 oz) tin pineapple (drain and
keep juice or syrup)

200 ml (7 fl oz) malt vinegar

2 tablespoons soy sauce

1 pepper red, yellow, green or mixed, chopp

1 tablespoon molasses, optional

RICE
375 g (12 oz) brown or white rice

METHOD

Croquettes - Beat the egg whites until stiff. In another bowl, combine the yolks, onion, parsley and cheese.
Mix well. Fold in the egg whites. Gradually add the oats. Form into 4 cm (1½ inch) balls (if it doesn't hold together, let it s
briefly). Roll in the oat flour to coat. Heat the oil in a heavy skillet. Brown the croquettes on all sides. Let the croquettes d
on paper to absorb the excess oil. Keep warm.

Sauce - Mix the cornflour and pineapple juice and pour into a saucepan. Stir in the honey/syrup, vinegar, molasses (option
and soy sauce until smooth. Cook over a medium heat until the mixture thickens and boils. Gently boil and stir for 1 minu
Add the pepper, pineapple and croquettes.

RICE - Cook the rice following the directions on the packet.

Serve the croquettes and sauce over the rice. Reserve some of the sauce to dispense as extra.

SERVES 5-6

NO: 54] LEEK & RED ONION COBBLER WITH POTATO CHEESE PASTRY

THE RT REV DAVID N DE L YOUNG, THE BISHOP OF RIPON

This is the Bishop's favourite dish for under £5.

INGREDIENTS

FILLING

1 kg (2 lb) leeks

25 g (1 oz) butter

2 teaspoons caraway seeds

Sea salt, to taste

2 large red onions

4 tablespoons extra virgin olive oil

4-5 pinches of chilli powder

PASTRY TOP

375 g (12 oz) potatoes

1 rounded teaspoon salt

150 g (5 oz) butter

1 tablespoon Parmesan cheese, grated

175 g (6 oz) self-raising flour

75 g (3 oz) strong flavoured cheese, grated

1 egg yolk

Oven - 200 °C, 400 F, Gas Mark 6

METHOD

To make the filling trim the leeks and cut into 2½ cm (1 inch) pieces using as much of the green part as possible. Peel the onions and chop into roughly 2½ cm (1 inch) pieces. Melt the butter with the olive oil in a large deep frying pan. Add the leeks and onions and caraway seeds. Cook over a medium heat, stirring fairly often, until the leeks and onions have softened. Season to taste with chilli powder and salt. Turn the filling into a large, shallow, ovenproof dish. Leave to cool while you make the pastry.

For the pastry, peel the potatoes and steam or boil them until they are soft. Mash them in a bowl until they are as smooth as possible and set aside until cold. Sift the flour and salt into another bowl. Stir in the grated cheese. Then add the butter, cut into small pieces, and rub with your fingertips until the mixture resembles rough breadcrumbs. Work in the cold mashed potato with your hands and knead the mixture to make a smooth dough. If you are not using the dough immediately, form it into a ball, wrap it in cling film and refrigerate.

When the leek mixture is cold, roll out the pastry to about 5 mm (¼ inch) thick on a floured board. Using a 5 cm (2 inch) biscuit cutter, cut the pastry into circles, re-rolling the scraps. Arrange the circles overlapping on top of the leek mixture. The dish can be refrigerated at this time until you are ready to cook.

Brush the pastry circles with egg yolk and sprinkle with the grated Parmesan cheese. Cook the cobbler in the centre of a pre-heated oven for 25-30 minutes until the pastry has turned a rich golden brown.

Serve with green vegetables.

(see photograph on p.98)

NO: 55] BEAN & VEGETABLE STEW WITH HERB DUMPLINGS

CHRISTINE HILL
MEMBER OF THE MUMS' GROUP OF ST. GEORGE'S CHURCH, LEEDS

INGREDIENTS

2 tablespoons oil

500 g (1 lb) leeks, chopped

250 g (8 oz) mushrooms, sliced

300 ml (1/2 pint) vegetable stock

1 tablespoon soy sauce

Salt and pepper, to taste

2 garlic cloves, crushed

1 large carrot, diced

400 g (14 oz) tin tomatoes

1 tablespoon paprika

430 g (15 1/4 oz) tin kidney beans

FOR THE DUMPLINGS

125 g (4 oz) self-raising flour

3 tablespoons chopped mixed fresh herbs

50 g (2 oz) vegetable suet

5 tablespoons cold water

METHOD

Heat the oil in a large saucepan. Add the garlic, leeks, carrots and mushrooms and sauté until just tender. Add the tomatoes and juice, stock, paprika and soy sauce. Bring to the boil and simmer for 20 minutes.

Meanwhile make the dumplings. Mix the flour, suet and herbs together. Add the water gradually to bring the mixture to a dough consistency. Roll the dumplings into rough round shapes.

Add the beans, salt and pepper to the stew. Arrange the dumplings on top. Cover and simmer for a further 20 minutes until the dumplings are cooked.

SERVES 4

NO: 56] BROAD BEANS WITH BREAD

MANAL BAKER KAROONI

SUPPORTER OF ST. GEORGE'S CRYPT, LEEDS

"Broad brown beans are one of the many kinds of beans used in middle eastern countries. This kind can be eaten as a snack, at breakfast, or as a main dish with khoubz (Arabic bread)."

INGREDIENTS

250 g (9 oz) dried broad brown beans

3 tablespoons olive oil or sunflower oil

3-4 pitta bread or 1-2 Arabic khoubz

Squeeze of lemon juice to serve

1 chilli pepper

1 medium-sized onion

Chopped parsley or mint to garnish

METHOD

Soak the broad beans overnight in plenty of cold water.

Rinse and drain the beans, put them into a large saucepan with the chilli and cover them with cold water. Boil rapidly for 10 minutes. Reduce the heat, cover and simmer for 1½-2 hours until tender, then add the salt. After the beans have been cooked, slice the onion into rings, sauté them in oil until soft and golden.

Meanwhile, cut the pitta bread into small pieces and arrange them in a bowl or deep plate. Soak the pieces by pouring the beans with their liquid on top (you can leave the beans with their skin or peel them). Pour the hot oil with the onions on top of the bread and beans. Garnish with chopped parsley or mint and a squeeze of lemon. Serve hot.

As an alternative, omit the bread, peel the beans, add olive oil with lemon juice and eat as a starter.

SERVES 4

NO: 57] SPINACH ROULADE *with mushroom & soured cream filling*

JANET GIBSON
ST. GEORGE'S CHURCH, LEEDS

INGREDIENTS

450 g (1 lb) frozen chopped spinach

Salt and pepper, to taste

A little grated Parmesan cheese

15 g (½ oz) margarine

4 eggs separated

FILLING

15 g (½ oz) margarine

275 ml (10 fl oz) soured cream

175 g (6 oz) button mushrooms, cleaned and sliced

Pinch of nutmeg, seasoning to taste

Oven - 200 °C, 400 F, Gas Mark 6

METHOD

Line a shallow swiss roll tin (18 cm x 28 cm, 7 inch x 11 inch) with greased greaseproof paper to cover the base and extend up each side.

Cook the spinach as per packet instructions and drain well. Add the margarine, salt, pepper and egg yolks. Sprinkle with the Parmesan cheese. Whisk the egg whites until stiff, but not dry. Fold them into the spinach mixture. Pour the mixture into the tin and bake in a pre-heated oven for 10-15 minutes until risen and springy to touch.

While the roulade is cooking, make the filling. Sauté the mushrooms quickly in the margarine over a high heat for 2-3 minutes. Add the cream, salt, pepper and nutmeg and heat gently without boiling. Take a large piece of greaseproof paper dusted with the cheese and turn out the roulade onto it. Strip off the first greaseproof. Spread the filling over the roulade, then roll it up and place in a warm ovenproof dish. Return to the oven for a further 5 minutes to heat through.

SERVES 4

(see photograph on p.99)

NO: 58] VEGETARIAN QUICHE

MARGARET ABBISS
ST. GEORGE'S CHURCH, LEEDS

INGREDIENTS

175 g (6 oz) short crust pastry (see section on basics)

1 tablespoon olive oil

3-4 slices green pepper, finely chopped

3-4 slices orange pepper, finely chopped

3-4 slices red pepper, finely chopped

1/4 red onion, finely chopped

1 large celery stick, chopped

275 g (10 oz) tin chopped tomatoes

1/4 apple, finely chopped

1 tablespoon raisins

2 eggs

2 tablespoons cottage cheese

2 tablespoons double cream

75g (3 oz) hard cheddar, grated

Oven - 200 °C, 400F, Gas Mark 6

METHOD

Grease a deep 23 cm (9 inch) tin and line with the pastry.

Heat the oil in a large pan or wok. Add the peppers, onion, celery, tomatoes, apple and raisins. Sauté until soft. Allow to cool a little and place in the pastry base.

Beat the eggs with the cottage cheese and double cream. Pour the mixture over the vegetables and sprinkle with the cheddar cheese. Bake in a pre-heated oven for about 30 minutes.

SERVES 4

"ST GEORGE'S CRYPT IS SO GOOD AT GETTING ME THROUGH MY BAD TIMES. THANK YOU FOR EVERYTHING, BUT MOST OF ALL THANK YOU FOR BEING THERE."
A REGULAR VISITOR TO THE NIGHT SOCIAL AND EMERGENCY CENTRE OF ST GEORGE'S CRYPT.

NO: 59] SAVOURY NUT ROAST

LORD RICHARD ATTENBOROUGH
ACTOR, FILM PRODUCER & DIRECTOR

INGREDIENTS

50 g (2 oz) walnuts, minced or liquidised

110 g (4 oz) brazil nuts, minced or liquidised

25 g (1 oz) butter or oil

2 eggs

1 level teaspoon mixed herbs or thyme

Salt and pepper, to taste

50 g (2 oz) cashew nuts, minced or liquidised

1 small onion, chopped

2 tablespoons wheatgerm, or 1 level tablespoon onion soup mix

4 oz tomatoes, skinned and sliced or 150 ml (5 fl oz) tinned tomatoes, drained

Oven - 180 °C, 350 F, Gas Mark 4

METHOD

Grease a 23 cm (9 inch) ovenproof dish or tin.

Sauté the onion in the butter or oil and remove from the heat. Remove the onion and set the butter or oil on one side. Mix the onion with all the other ingredients. Press into the dish or tin and brush the top with the melted butter or oil.

Bake in a pre-heated oven on the top shelf for about 40 minutes, or until brown. Serve hot with gravy or onion sauce, vegetables and potatoes. Alternatively, serve cold sliced with salad, chips or rolls and butter.

SERVES 4

NO: 60] MORAVIAN POTATO PANCAKES

MIRIAM SLECHTA
ST. GEORGE'S CHURCH, LEEDS

INGREDIENTS

3 medium-sized potatoes, well washed

1 egg

2 heaped teaspoons mixed herbs or marjoram

teaspoon caraway seeds (optional)

1 medium-sized onion

3-4 heaped tablespoons plain flour

1 level teaspoon salt

2 (or more) garlic cloves, crushed

3-4 teaspoons vegetable oil (for frying)

Cheddar cheese (optional)

METHOD

Grate (either coarse or fine) the unpeeled potatoes into a large bowl. Grate the onion and add to the potatoes. Add, and mix, all the above ingredients (except oil) into the bowl.

Heat the vegetable oil in a large frying pan. Spread half the mixture evenly onto the pan. Fry it slowly until golden brown. Turn it over and fry the other side in the same way. Then repeat the process for the other half of the mixture.

Serve warm and plain on a plate, or with more crushed garlic spread on the top. Alternatively, cut thin slices of cheddar cheese and put them on top of the pancake. Grill until the cheese just melts.

Serve hot, ideally with lemon or herb tea.

SERVES 1-2

NO: 61] MASALA POTATO

PAULINE NELSON
MEMBER OF THE MUMS' GROUP OF ST. GEORGE'S CHURCH, LEEDS

"This South Indian spicy potato dish is served with the thin rice pancakes called Dosai, but it is delicious with a wide variety of foods, e.g. to add interest to an otherwise bland meal."

INGREDIENTS

6 small/medium potatoes, peeled or not according to preference

1/2 teaspoon ground ginger or grated fresh ginger

1/2 teaspoon curry powder

1 small fresh chilli pepper, chopped

1 green pepper, chopped small

250 ml (9 fl oz) buttermilk

A little fresh chopped mint (optional)

80 ml (3 fl oz) vegetable oil

1/2 teaspoon turmeric

2 teaspoons salt

1 large onion, finely chopped

2 garlic cloves

50 g (2 oz) unsweetened coconut, shredded

METHOD

Boil the potatoes until just tender, then cut into cubes 1-2 cm (1/2-1 inch).

Heat the oil in a separate pan, then add the ginger, turmeric, curry powder, salt, chilli pepper, onion, green pepper and garlic. Sauté until the onion is soft. Add the potato and mix gently. Cover and cook over a low heat for 10 minutes.

Mix the buttermilk with the coconut and chopped mint (optional). Add to the potato and cook until just blended and warmed through.

SERVES 4-6 AS A SIDE DISH

NO: 62] ROASTED GREEK SALAD

WITH PERMISSION OF GOOD HOUSEKEEPING

INGREDIENTS

225 g (8 oz) feta cheese

1/2 teaspoon balsamic or red wine vinegar

2 level tablespoons chopped fresh thyme

700 g (1½ lb) tomatoes

4 garlic cloves

50 g (2 oz) pitted black olives

2 tablespoons olive oil

1 tablespoon lemon juice

Black pepper, to taste

900 g (2 lb) courgettes

225 g (8 oz) small red onions

Oven - 230 °C, 450 F, Gas Mark 8

marinating time - 1 hour

METHOD

Slice the feta cheese into 1 cm (½ inch) thick pieces. Mix together half the olive oil, the balsamic vinegar, lemon juice and half the chopped thyme. Season with plenty of black pepper. Pour over the feta and leave to marinate for at least 1 hour.

Halve or quarter the tomatoes, thickly slice the courgettes, thinly slice the garlic cloves and quarter the onions. Place the courgettes, garlic and onions in a roasting tin with the remaining olive oil. Cook in the oven for 30 minutes turning occasionally. Add the tomatoes, olives and remaining thyme. Cook for 10 minutes or until the vegetables are tender. Season.

Just before the end of the cooking time, drain the cheese from the marinade and place on a baking sheet in an oven for about 5-7 minutes or until bubbling and slightly browned.

Serve the roasted vegetables with the remaining marinade and topped with feta cheese.

SERVES 4

Variation - For a tasty alternative, substitute roughly chopped aubergine and onion for half the courgettes and tomatoes. Add with the courgettes.

Cook's Tip - Use a fish slice to move the feta so that it doesn't break up. We recommend seasoning with black pepper only as feta cheese is very salty.

© GOODHOUSEKEEPING 1994

NO: 63] GIRL FRIDAY'S LIME RICE

JOANNA LUMLEY
ACTRESS

INGREDIENTS

2 mugs basmati rice

Juice of 4 ripe limes

1 vegetable stock cube

4 cardamom pods, optional

METHOD

Dissolve the stock cube in a large pan of water and boil. Add the rice and cardamoms. Boil the rice until cooked, i.e. until there is a pinprick of white in the centre of a bitten grain. Drain and put in a covered sieve over an inch of practically boiling water for 3 minutes to steam dry.

Serve as an accompaniment to vegetable curry, drenched in the juice of the limes.

SERVES 4-6

> "OH, IT WAS WONDERFUL - THEY TOOK ME IN, LET ME HAVE A HOT BATH, AND SET ABOUT FINDING A PLACE FOR ME. I DIDN'T KNOW PEOPLE LIKE THAT EXISTED." **- A GRATEFUL HOMELESS PERSON**

NO: 64] ANGLESEY EGGS

GLENYS KINNOCK
LABOUR MEP FOR SOUTH WALES EAST

"My Anglesey grandmother often used to make this for supper. It is suitable for vegetarians too."

INGREDIENTS

8 eggs	700 g (1½ lb) potatoes
6 leeks	25 g (1 oz) butter
Salt and pepper, to taste	75 g (3 oz) grated (Welsh) cheese

WHITE SAUCE

25 g (1 oz) plain flour	25 g (1 oz) butter or margarine
275 ml (½ pint) milk	Salt and pepper, to taste

Oven - 200 °C, 400 F, Gas Mark 6

METHOD

Hard boil the eggs. Cut the leeks into rings and boil in salted water for 10 minutes. (I always microwave leeks and find this is much better) Boil and mash the potatoes and then add the leeks, seasoning and butter. Mix together.

To make the white sauce, melt the butter or margarine in a saucepan and stir in the flour over a low heat. Gradually add the milk, stirring with a wooden spoon all the time, until the sauce comes to the boil and thickens. Add most of the cheese and let the sauce cook for a further 5 minutes and season to taste.

Arrange the mashed potato mixture around the edge of a large dish. Put the eggs in the middle. Pour the cheese sauce over the ingredients and sprinkle the remaining cheese over the top. (I like to crumble Caerphilly cheese.) Bake in the oven for 20 minutes until the top is golden.

Serve with vegetables or a mixed salad - arddferchog!

SERVES 4

DESSERTS

NO: 65] BLACK & WHITE GATEAU

PAM RHODES

BBC TV PRESENTER OF 'SONGS OF PRAISE'

"Many moons ago, I was a member of the Black and White Minstrels and the following recipe is a gateau that a group of us invented for a party we organised. It is delightfully soggy, unashamedly fattening, and unspeakably delicious! Not only that, but it's a piece of cake to make!"

INGREDIENTS

2 round plain sponge cakes

2 tablespoons boiling water

275 ml (10 fl oz) double cream

1 level tablespoon instant coffee

2 tablespoons brandy

2-3 tablespoons flaked almonds

METHOD

Lay out the 2 sponge cakes. (I always do this on silver foil, so that I can curl it up at the edges - you don't want to lose any of the drips!) Dissolve the coffee in the boiling water, and add the brandy. Spoon the mixture on to both sides of the cakes, soaking thoroughly. You may need to add a bit more liquid, if you like it really soggy. The finished effect should be almost marbled - the moist coffee-flavoured cake contrasting against the original yellow sponge.

Whip the cream. Lightly toast the almond flakes until golden brown. Place one sponge cake on a serving plate and cover the sides and top completely with the cream. Layer some of the toasted almonds on top of this first layer of cake. Then add the second cake, coating completely once again in cream. Cover the top and the sides of the gateau with toasted almond flakes. It might help to leave the final cover of almond flakes until just before you serve the gateau, so that they are still crisp. Eat with a spoon!

SERVES 6-8

NO: 66] TRANSKEI MUD

SIR CLIFF RICHARD
SINGER, ENTERTAINER & PATRON OF THE 'MORE THAN A ROOF' APPEAL

INGREDIENTS

1 tin condensed milk

200-225 g (7-8 oz) digestive biscuits, crushed if preferred

275 ml (10 fl oz) double cream

2 flat blocks mint chocolate (Aero or Bitz)

prepare 2 days before serving

METHOD

To caramelise the condensed milk, boil the tin - unopened and well-covered with water in a saucepan with a lid - for about 2 hours. Allow to cool overnight, in a refrigerator.

Whisk the double cream until thick. Slowly add the caramelised condensed milk, one spoonful at a time. Mix together thoroughly. Grate 1½ blocks of the mint chocolate into the mixture and stir in. Grate the remaining chocolate and reserve for garnish.

Layer the mixture in a dish or individual serving dishes, alternating with the biscuits - 3 layers of each. Keep in a refrigerator overnight.

Garnish with grated mint chocolate before serving.

SERVES 6-8

NO: 67] THE DEAN'S CREAM

JANET GIBSON
ST. GEORGE'S CHURCH, LEEDS

"Always popular at dinner parties."

INGREDIENTS

8 trifle sponges

50 g (2 oz) ratafia biscuits

150 ml (5 fl oz) sherry

3 tablespoons brandy

300 ml (10 fl oz) whipping cream

100 g (4 oz) jam of your choice

Grated rind and juice of 1 lemon

3 tablespoons white wine

50 g (2 oz) caster sugar

Flaked almonds (optional)

Prepare 1 day in advance

METHOD

Split the trifle sponges and sandwich them together with the jam. Layer the sponges in a deep dish. Scatter the ratafias over the sponges and then soak with sherry.

Place the lemon rind and lemon juice in a saucepan with the sugar. Warm gently to dissolve the sugar. Then add the wine and brandy. Remove from the heat and leave to cool.

Whip the cream until thick, then fold into the cooled wine mixture. Spoon the cream mixture over the sponge cakes and chill for several hours or overnight. Decorate with flaked almonds just before serving, if liked.

SERVES 6-8

NO: 68] BLACK FOREST TRIFLE

CILLA BLACK
TV PRESENTER & ENTERTAINER

INGREDIENTS

250 g (9 oz) sponge cake or 1 packet trifle sponges

425 g (15 oz) tin pitted cherries

175 g (6 oz) double cream

A few glacé cherries for decoration

1 Rowntree's black cherry jelly

570 ml (1 pint) custard

A dash of cherry brandy or sherry

1 Cadbury's Flake or Jordan's apple crunch

METHOD

Line the base of the trifle bowl with the sponge cake and soak in the juice from the tin of cherries, together with a good dash of cherry brandy or sherry. Make the black cherry jelly, according to the instructions on the packet. Pour it on top of the sponge and mix in the pitted cherries. Allow to set.

Make the thick custard with the custard powder, or for real luxury, make an egg custard. Pour on top of the jelly.

When the custard has cooled, whisk up the double cream and pipe on top. Sprinkle with the flake and decorate with glacé cherries.

Jordan's apple crunch is also tasty sprinkled on the cream instead of the Flake.

Serve when completely set.

SERVES 8

NO: 69] NUTTY MERINGUE

ANN WEIR
ST. GEORGE'S CHURCH, LEEDS

"Scrumptious."

INGREDIENTS

4 egg whites

1/2 teaspoon vanilla essence

125 g (4 1/2 oz) toasted hazelnuts or chopped nuts

275 g (10 oz) caster sugar

1 teaspoon vinegar

FILLING

275 ml (10 fl oz) double cream, whipped

250 g (9 oz) raspberries

1 tablespoon caster sugar

Oven - 150 °C, 300 F, Gas Mark 2

METHOD

Meringue - Grease and line two 20 cm (8 inch) flat round tins. Alternatively, cut out two 21 cm (8 1/2 inch) circles of greaseproof paper, place on a baking sheet, and brush with oil. Whisk the egg whites until stiff. Whisk in the sugar a little at a time. When the meringue is stiff and holds its shape, fold in the vanilla essence, vinegar and nuts.

Divide the mixture between the sheets. Bake in a pre-heated oven for up to 40 minutes.

Leave to cool for 2 minutes before removing from the tins, and turn onto wire racks. When cool remove the paper.

Filling - Mix the cream, raspberries and sugar together. Sandwich the meringue rounds together with the mixture.

SERVES 8

"I AM 17. I'VE BEEN ON THE STREETS OR IN AND OUT OF FRIENDS' HOUSES SINCE I WAS 15. I CAN'T GET ANY MONEY FROM SOCIAL SECURITY. WHAT I WANT IS TO HAVE SOMEWHERE OF MY OWN, GET A JOB AND LOOK AFTER MYSELF. THAT ISN'T TOO MUCH TO ASK IS IT?"
USER OF ST GEORGE'S CRYPT NIGHT SOCIAL AND EMERGENCY CENTRE

NO: 70] CRÈME BRULÉE

MARGARET MASON

ST. GEORGE'S CHURCH, LEEDS

"A light but delicious dessert, very easy to make."

INGREDIENTS

4 egg yolks

300 ml (10 fl oz) double cream

Few drops vanilla essence

50 ml (2 fl oz) water

50 g (2 oz) caster sugar

300 ml (10 fl oz) single cream

75 g (3 oz) granulated sugar

Oven - 150 °C, 300 F, Gas Mark 2

Prepare 1 day in advance

METHOD

Blend the egg yolks and the caster sugar. Pour the cream onto the egg mixture and stir in the vanilla essence. Put the mixture into an ovenproof dish and place in a tin containing an inch of water. Bake until firm, usually about 1 hour, and allow to cool. Leave overnight in a refrigerator.

Next day, make the caramel. Brush a baking tray with oil. Put the granulated sugar and water in a pan and dissolve over a low heat. Boil rapidly (be careful as it will burn very easily) until pale and caramel in colour. Immediately pour three quarters over the custard and the rest onto the oiled tray. When set, crush and place around the edge of the custard in the dish.

SERVES 4

NO: 71] RASPBERRY BLISS

GILL SMITH
MEMBER OF MUMS' GROUP OF ST. GEORGE'S CHURCH, LEEDS

"This pudding is a firm favourite with my family and is very quick and easy to make."

INGREDIENTS

425 g (15 oz) fresh or frozen raspberries

175 g (6 oz) caster sugar

1 tablespoon sherry

275 ml (10 fl oz) double cream

175 g (6 oz) fresh brown breadcrumbs

40 g (1½ oz) plain chocolate, grated,
plus a little extra for decoration

METHOD

Mix the breadcrumbs, sugar and chocolate together. Place a layer of raspberries (reserving some for decoration) in the bottom of a suitable serving dish. Add a layer of crumb mixture followed by another layer of raspberries and yet another layer of crumb mixture.

Whisk the cream until thick (not too stiff) and add the sherry. Decorate the pudding with cream, grated chocolate and raspberries.

Leave overnight in a refrigerator to allow the raspberries to soak into the crumb mixture.

SERVES 6

(see photograph on p.102)

NO: 72] PASSION FRUIT WATER ICE

SALLY GUNNELL
WOMEN'S 400 M HURDLES WORLD RECORD HOLDER (1993)
& OLYMPIC (1992) & WORLD CHAMPIONSHIP (1993) GOLD MEDALLIST

INGREDIENTS

570 ml (1 pint) water

1 egg white

225 g (8 oz) caster sugar

8 passion fruits

METHOD

Dissolve the sugar in the water over a low heat. Boil gently for 10 minutes. Leave to cool. Cut the passion fruits in half and scoop out the flesh. Put into a fine sieve and pass through leaving all the black pips behind.

Add the juice to the cooled sugar syrup and pour into a container. Place in the freezer and leave until just beginning to freeze around the edges. Add the whisked egg white and return to the freezer.

I serve this delicious water ice in pretty wine glasses with a wafer biscuit on top.

NO: 73] LEMON MALLOW PIE

CILBIE APPLEYARD
ST. GEORGE'S CHURCH, LEEDS

"Appearance similar to cheese cake, but more economical. Delicious"

INGREDIENTS

50 g (2 oz) butter

50 g (2 oz) demerara sugar

150 ml (1/4 pint) boiled water for the jelly

1 large tin evaporated milk

175 g (6 oz) digestive biscuits, crushed

1 packet lemon jelly

1 lemon

1 chocolate flake

METHOD

Grease a 20 cm (8 inch) pie dish. Place the biscuit crumbs in a bowl and add the sugar. Melt the butter in a pan, add to the biscuits and mix well. Press into the bottom and sides of the pie dish.

Cut the jelly into cubes, add 150 ml (1/4pint) boiled water and stir until the jelly is dissolved. Thinly grate the lemon rind and add to the liquid. Blend the lemon flesh (discard the pith) with the jelly thoroughly, until well mixed. Strain into a bowl, then add the evaporated milk. Mix well.

Pour into the biscuit crumb pie shell. Leave in a cool place to set.

Decorate with the chocolate flake and serve cold.

SERVES 6

"I NEEDED SOMEWHERE SAFE AND I KNEW ST GEORGE'S CRYPT WOULD TRY TO HELP ME SORT OUT MY PROBLEMS."
USER OF ST. GEORGE'S CRYPT NIGHT SOCIAL AND EMERGENCY CENTRE.

NO: 74] CHEESECAKE SUPREMO

EDITH GOLDSPINK
ST GEORGE'S CHURCH, LEEDS

"Simply scrumptious - a rich and delightfully creamy cheescake extremely easy to make. Delicious, but definitely not for the calorie conscious!"

INGREDIENTS

BASE

220 g (8 oz) digestive biscuits

6 tablespoons Nutella chocolate hazlenut spread

FILLING

450 g (1 lb) full fat soft cheese

3 medium eggs, slightly beaten

110 g (4 oz) melted butter

125 g (5 oz) castor sugar

25 g (1 oz) flour

150 ml (5 fl oz) sour cream

2 teaspoons vanilla essence

300 ml (10 fl oz) double cream - for decoration

Chocolate - for decoration

Oven - 180 °C, 350 F, Gas Mark 4

METHOD

Grease an 18 cm (9 inch) loose-bottomed cake tin.

Crush the biscuits and mix with the Nutella spread. Press firmly into the cake tin and put in a refrigerator. Put all the other ingredients into a food processor and mix until smooth. Pour into the cake tin and cook for 1 hour until firm.

Whip the double cream until firm and spread over the top of the cheesecake.

Decorate with pieces/flakes/swirls of chocolate.

SERVES 8

see recipe on p.75

see recipe on p.78

NO: 75] BANOFFI PIE

GARY LINEKER

PRESENTER OF FOOTBALL PROGRAMMES ON BBC TV. FORMER CAPTAIN (1990-1992)
& MEMBER OF THE ENGLAND FOOTBALL TEAM, WITH 80 APPEARANCES BETWEEN 1984 & 1992

He just loves the taste!

INGREDIENTS

175 g (6 oz) short crust pastry (see section on basics)

1 level teaspoon powdered instant coffee

150 ml (5 fl oz) double cream

1 tin condensed milk

25 g (1 oz) caster sugar

1 large banana, sliced

METHOD

The really clever bit of this recipe lies in the condensed milk.

Immerse the tin UNOPENED in boiling water. Cover and boil for 3 hours (keep it covered otherwise it will explode!). Remove from the water and allow to cool completely before opening. Inside you will find the soft toffee filling for this pie.

Now take a 20 cm (8 inch) flan tin. Grease and line it with a thin layer of short crust pastry. Bake it blind until crisp (you can use baking beans to help the pastry keep its shape, if you want). Leave to cool.

Whip the cream with the coffee and sugar until thick and smooth. Empty the toffee mixture into the flan case. Spread evenly across the bottom. Layer the sliced banana over the top. Cover with the cream, either dollop it on with a spoon or, if you are showing off, pipe it on in pretty patterns. Either way it tastes delicious.

SERVES 6-8

NO: 76] PARADISE PUMPKIN PIE

MRS BILLY GRAHAM

WIFE OF THE INTERNATIONAL EVANGELIST & WRITER

INGREDIENTS

225 g (8 oz) packet cream cheese

1/2 teaspoon vanilla essence

350 g (12 oz) shortcrust pastry (see section on handy basics)

50 g (2 oz) caster sugar

1 egg

FILLING

325 g (12 oz) tin pumpkin

1 teaspoon cinnamon

1/4 teaspoon nutmeg

2 eggs, slightly beaten

Maple syrup, nuts or whipped cream to serve

100 g (4 oz) caster sugar

1/4 teaspoon ginger

250 ml (9 fl oz) evaporated milk

Dash of salt

Oven - 180 °C, 350 F, Gas Mark 4

METHOD

Grease two 20 cm (8 inch) pie tins and line each with the pastry.

Combine the cheese, sugar and vanilla. Add the eggs and mix well. Spread evenly between the tins.

Combine the remaining ingredients and mix well. Carefully pour over the cream cheese mixture. Cook for about 1 hour, or until done (when a sharp knife inserted into the pie comes out clean).

Cool. If desired, brush with maple syrup and garnish with nuts, or serve with whipped cream.

MAKES 2 PIES

see recipe on p. 94

see recipe on p.105

NO: 77] RHUBARB MERINGUE

PADDY McCLEAN

ST. GEORGE'S CHURCH, LEEDS

INGREDIENTS

250 g (9 oz) short crust pastry (see section on handy basics)

FILLING

450 g (1 lb) rhubarb   110 g (4 oz) caster sugar

35 g (1¼ oz) flour   2 egg yolks

MERINGUE

2 egg whites   110 g (4 oz) caster sugar

Oven - See text below

METHOD

Grease a 20 cm (8 inch) sandwich cake tin. Line the tin with the pastry.

Bake blind with baking beans on a high shelf at 190 °C, 375 F, Gas Mark 5 for 15-20 minutes.

Filling - Chop the rhubarb into 1 cm (½ inch) pieces. Cream the egg yolks and sugar together, add the flour and then the rhubarb. Transfer to a pastry case.

Bake at 200 °C, 400 F, Gas Mark 6 for 10-15 minutes, then reduce the temperature to 180 °C, 350 F, Gas Mark 4 and continue baking for about 20-25 minutes, until the rhubarb is soft.

Meringue - Beat the egg whites until stiff. Add the sugar a little at time folding in to the egg whites after each addition. Spread over the rhubarb filling, peak with a fork, and bake on the middle shelf, until the meringue turns pale brown on the peaks; approximately 10-15 minutes at 180 °C, 350 F, Gas Mark 4.

SERVES 6

NO: 78] FRENCH PEAR TART

VIVIENNE CLARKE

MEMBER OF MUMS' GROUP OF ST. GEORGE'S CHURCH, LEEDS

"This has been a family favourite for many years."

INGREDIENTS

PASTRY
170 g (6 oz) flour
75 g (3 oz) butter
2 egg yolks

Pinch of salt
50 g (2 oz) caster sugar

FILLING
2 ripe pears
110 g (4 oz) caster sugar
2 teaspoons brandy
2-3 drops almond essence

110 g (4 oz) butter
1 egg and 1 egg yolk (medium-sized eggs)
110 g (4 oz) ground almonds
25 g (1 oz) plain flour

TOPPING
Caster sugar to sprinkle

Glaze (optional)
3-4 tablespoons apricot jam

Oven - 200 °C, 400 F, Gas Mark 6 for 15 minutes
180 °C, 350 F, Gas Mark 4 for 15-20 minutes

METHOD

Grease a 23 cm (9 inch) loose-bottomed flan tin. Sift the flour and salt into a bowl. Rub in the butter until the mixture resembles fine breadcrumbs. Add the sugar then the egg yolks and 2-3 tablespoons of water to form a smooth dough. Place in a refrigerator for 30 minutes.

Roll out the pastry, line the tin, prick with a fork and chill while you make the filling.

Pre-heat the oven. Cream the butter and sugar until light and fluffy. Add the egg and yolk, then the brandy, ground almonds, almond essence and the flour and mix together. Spread this mixture over the pastry base. Then peel, core and halve the pears and cut into thin slices. Arrange these slices in the flan, like the spokes of a wheel or in concentric circles and press the slices down.

Bake in the oven for 15 minutes, then reduce the heat and bake for a further 15-20 minutes until the filling is set. When hot, sprinkle with caster sugar. If you want a glaze, brush with the jam while the tart is warm.

(see photograph on p.103)

see recipe on p.128, 125 & 117

Photography & copyright Andrew Walton Vaines, see recipe on p.150, 151 & 152

NO: 79] PANCAKE PARCELS

HRH THE DUCHESS OF KENT

Her Royal Highness is pleased to contribute one of her favourite recipes to this cookbook.

INGREDIENTS

PANCAKE MIXTURE

110 g (4 oz) plain flour

1 egg

Vegetable oil for frying

Pinch of salt

300 ml (10 fl oz) milk

FILLING

3 medium bananas

2 tablespoons apricot jam

Juice of 1 small lemon

SAUCE

4 tablespoons undiluted orange squash

1/2 teaspoon ground cinnamon

2 tablespoons soft brown sugar

Cream to serve

METHOD

Pancake Mixture - Sift the flour and salt into a bowl and make a well in the centre. Add the egg and gradually beat in the milk, drawing in the flour from the sides to make a smooth batter.

Heat a little oil in a frying pan until very hot. Pour in a few spoonfuls of the batter, tilting the pan so that it spreads evenly and cook until golden brown. Turn over the pancake and cook the underneath until golden brown. Remove from the pan and keep hot while frying the remaining batter, making 8 pancakes in all.

Filling - Peel the bananas and mash the flesh with the lemon juice and jam. Divide the filling equally between the pancakes. Fold each pancake around the filling to make a 'parcel'.

Sauce - Make the orange squash up to 150 ml (1/4 pt) with water and then pour into a large frying pan. Add the remaining ingredients, excluding the cream, and bring to the boil, stirring constantly. Boil for 5 minutes until reduced, then lower the heat.

Arrange the pancake parcels in a single layer in the pan, then heat through for about 10 minutes, spooning the sauce over the pancakes from time to time.

Serve hot, with cream.

MAKES 8

NO: 80] APPLE TURNOVERS

LINFORD CHRISTIE

MEN'S 100M OLYMPIC (1992) & WORLD CHAMPIONSHIP (1993) GOLD MEDALLIST

INGREDIENTS

440 g (14 oz) stewed apple-
-(or unsweetened tinned apple pie filling)
Sugar to taste
50 g (2 oz) sultanas

12 slices of bread
40 g (1½ oz) ground cinnamon
12 toothpicks

GLAZE
1 tablespoon honey

1 tablespoon hot water

Oven - 180 °C, 350 F, Gas Mark 5

METHOD

Cut the crusts off the bread and flatten each slice with a rolling pin.

Mix the apple, sugar, cinnamon and sultanas together in a bowl. Place a spoonful of the mixture in the centre of each slice of bread. Now bring two opposite corners together and hold them in place with a toothpick.

Mix the honey and water together until the honey dissolves, then brush on to each bread parcel. Bake for 10-15 minutes or until golden and crisp.

SERVES 12

> "ME, I JUST NEED MY OWN PLACE THAT I CAN CALL HOME. EVEN IF IT'S ONLY ONE ROOM."
> **A YOUNG HOMELESS PERSON.**

NO: 81] BREAD & BUTTER & CINNAMON PUDDING

ALAN BENNETT
DRAMATIST & ACTOR

© David Hockney 94

INGREDIENTS

8 slices bread

2 eggs

570 ml (1 pint) milk

1-2 tablespoons soft brown sugar

1 mug breadcrumbs

75 g (3 oz) sultanas

3 tablespoons caster sugar

1 small tin evaporated milk

2 teaspoons cinnamon

Oven - See text below

METHOD

Grease a large, deep ovenproof dish. Lavishly butter the bread and layer in the dish with plenty of sultanas sprinkled between the layers. Beat the 2 eggs and 3 tablespoons of sugar together with a little milk. Add the evaporated milk plus a pint of ordinary milk, or as much as you need to fill the dish. Pour over the bread and leave to soak for 30 minutes.

Mix the breadcrumbs with the brown sugar and cinnamon. Spread the mixture over the top of the pudding and cover with foil. Cook at 140 °C, 275 F, Gas Mark 1 for 60 minutes. Remove the foil and cook at 150 °C, 300 F, Gas Mark 3 for a further 30 minutes or until the pudding has risen and is brown.

SERVES 6-8

Sponsored by The Asda Foundation

Young homeless – emotional and practical support

Photographs courtesy of Peter Langford, Yorkshire Evening Post

Creative skills shine through
and are encouraged

St. George's Crypt, Leeds
the family centre

This centre opens daily to provide practical support and friendship to low-income families. In an atmosphere of love and acceptance we encourage self-help and sharing so that people do not feel alone in their struggles and are able to preserve emotional and family stability. For a small donation parents can obtain clothing, bedding, crockery and other small household items. Educational classes cover budgeting, health issues, good parenting, child safety, etc.

Involvement in the day-to-day running of the Family Centre, coffee mornings, book weeks and fundraising activities encourage teamwork, helping parents to improve their social skills and self image. A playroom provides parents with a break from the constant demands of their young families. Each Christmas we give out new toys to some 700 needy children.

A family prayer (by Paul Leingang)

Lord God
You are Father and Mother to us;
our life begins in You.
You chose to make Your home among us.
You sent your Son to be one with us,
and Your Spirit to be with us forever.
Bless this home,
and Your people who live here.
Be here today,
as You were yesterday.
Be here tomorrow.
Be our shelter,
our walls to protect us.
Be our windows;
let us see the world through You.
Be our warmth,
to share with all who come in
and all who go forth.

Pancake Day.
Celebrated by women
who visit the family centre

HOME BAKING
& PRESERVES

No: 82] EASY APPLE CAKE

PAM PATERSON

PAM'S LATE HUSBAND, REVD. DON PATERSON WAS WARDEN OF ST. GEORGE'S CRYPT, LEEDS FOR OVER 20 YEARS. PAM HERSELF WAS A VOLUNTEER/STAFF MEMBER FOR MANY YEARS.

"A quick, easy and economical dessert suitable for a special occasion"

INGREDIENTS

300 g (11 oz) Madeira or plain cake

500 g (18 oz) baking apples

A little water

1 tablespoon lemon or orange juice (optional)

Icing to dust

60 g (2½ oz) butter

50 g (2 oz) sugar

25 g (1 oz) sultanas

A little cinnamon powder (optional)

Cream, ice-cream or custard to serve

Oven - 190 °C, 375 F, Gas Mark 5

METHOD

Grease and line a loose-bottomed 17 cm (7 inch) cake tin.

Gently stew the apples with the sugar and water until soft. Remove from the heat and stir in the sultanas and cinnamon. Melt the butter in a saucepan, crumble the cake and add to the butter, stirring well until evenly absorbed. Add the orange or lemon juice.

Put alternate layers of cake mix and apple into the cake tin, beginning and ending with cake mix. Do 5 or 7 layers in all. Press down well.

Bake in a pre-heated oven for about 25 minutes, until the top is crispy brown and firm. Cool, then remove on to a plate.

Sprinkle with icing sugar, prior to serving hot or cold with cream, ice-cream or custard.

SERVES 8

NO: 83] APPLE SHORTCAKE

DICKIE BIRD

FORMER INTERNATIONAL CRICKET UMPIRE
& PATRON OF THE 'MORE THAN A ROOF' APPEAL

"A lovely easy-to-make dessert."

INGREDIENTS

110 g (4 oz) margarine

175 g (6 oz) self-raising flour

450 g (1 lb) cooking apples, sugar to taste

75 g (3 oz) caster sugar

1 egg, beaten

Oven - 170 °C, 325 F, Gas Mark 3

METHOD

Grease an 18 cm (7 inch) square cake tin.

Peel, core and slice the apples. Cook in a pan with sufficient water to cover (add sugar to taste), until just soft. Drain and cool completely.

Cream the margarine with the sugar, then add the beaten egg. Gradually mix in the flour adding no liquid. Put half the mixture into the tin and level. Spread the apples over the mixture and cover with the remaining shortcake.

Bake in the oven for 1 hour, or until golden brown. When cold, cut into squares and dredge with icing sugar.

NO: 84] MARMALADE CAKE

LINDSEY PALLANT
ST. GEORGE'S CHURCH, LEEDS

INGREDIENTS

350 g (12 oz) self-raising flour

175 g (6 oz) caster sugar

1 heaped tablespoon marmalade

175-225 g (6-8 oz) mixed dried fruit

125-150 ml (4-5 fl oz) milk

Pinch of salt

175 g (6 oz) margarine

1 dessertspoon golden syrup

1 egg

Oven - 170 °C, 325 F, Gas Mark 3

METHOD

Grease and flour a 20 cm (8 inch) cake tin.

Sift the flour and salt into a bowl and stir in the sugar. Rub in the margarine and add the mixed fruit. Make a well in the centre of the mixture and add the beaten egg, marmalade, syrup and milk. Mix into a medium consistency. If it is too stiff it will not rise, so add more milk if necessary.

Place in the cake tin and bake for 1½ -2 hours.

"THE FAMILY CENTRE IN THE CRYPT IS A PLACE TO COME TO HAVE A CHAT WITH THE STAFF. THEY ARE THE FRIENDLIEST AND MOST HELPFUL PEOPLE AND MAKE YOU FEEL WELCOME AND AT HOME. THEY, AND A CUP OF TEA OR COFFEE, MAKE EVERYTHING WORTHWHILE." - A SATISFIED USER OF THE FAMILY CENTRE RUN BY ST. GEORGE'S CRYPT.

NO: 85] BANANA BREAD

EILEEN CAREY

WIFE OF THE ARCHBISHOP OF CANTERBURY, GEORGE CAREY

"It is a very cheap recipe and one can often pick up soft, over-ripe bananas from the greengrocers at a very low cost, and they are ideal for this recipe. It can be used as a pudding with yoghurt or cream, so it is not just a sliced cake."

INGREDIENTS

110 g (4 oz) margarine

1 egg

225 g (8 oz) self-raising flour

1 teaspoon vanilla essence

225 g (8 oz) caster sugar

3 large, soft, ripe bananas

1 teaspoon baking soda

50 g (2 oz) walnuts, chopped

Oven - 180 °C, 350 F, Gas Mark 4

METHOD

Liberally grease a medium-sized loaf tin and sprinkle with flour.

Cream the margarine and sugar. Add the beaten egg and mashed bananas and mix well.

Add the flour and baking soda and mix well. Add the vanilla essence and walnuts. Pour into the loaf tin and bake for approximately 60 minutes.

(see photograph on p.106)

NO: 86] BULGARIAN YOGHURT CAKE

JANE BARLOW

MISSION PARTNER OF ST. GEORGE'S CHURCH, LEEDS

"Very easy because you don't need scales and very versatile because you can vary the dried fruit and flavourings according to preference."

INGREDIENTS *(the yoghurt pot is used as the measure)*

150 ml (5 fl oz) pot natural set yoghurt, Bulgarian or Greek, if available

1 pot caster sugar

1/2 pot vegetable oil

1 pot cornflour

3 pinches salt

3 tablespoons Cognac/Cointreau or other preferred flavouring

1 1/2 pots candied/dried fruit according to taste - I use dried apricots, chopped

3 medium eggs, beaten

1 teaspoon vanilla essence

2 pots plain flour

1 teaspoon baking powder

Oven - 200 °C, 400 F, Gas Mark 6

METHOD

Grease and line a deep 20 cm (8 inch) cake tin.

Mix together in this order: the natural yoghurt, the beaten eggs, sugar, vanilla essence and the oil.

Then in another bowl, mix together the salt, flour, cornflour and baking powder and add to the liquid above. According to taste, add the liqueur and the fruit. Pour into the prepared cake tin and bake for 30 minutes.

This cake is best eaten within 2 days. May be frozen.

NO: 87] AUNTY MAY'S BOILED FRUIT CAKE

MAY SMITH

SUPPORTER OF ST. GEORGE'S CRYPT, LEEDS

INGREDIENTS

450 g (1 lb) dried fruit

175 g (6 oz) soft brown sugar

275 g (10 oz) self-raising flour, sieved

175 g (6 oz) margarine

275 ml (1/2 pint) water

2 eggs, beaten

Oven - 170 °C, 325 F, Gas Mark 3

METHOD

Grease and line a deep 23 cm (9 inch) square tin or two 17 cm (7 inch) square tins.

Place the dried fruit, margarine, sugar and water into a saucepan. Bring to the boil and then turn down to simmer for 15 minutes. Leave to cool for 15 minutes.

Stir in the beaten eggs with a wooden spoon and fold in the flour with a metal spoon. Place the mixture in the tin, pushing well into the corners and bake for 1-1½ hours (or 30-40 minutes for 2 tins), until firm to the touch and browned on top. Test with a skewer.

"WHEN MY LIFE SEEMS JUST SO USELESS I JUST PUT ON MY COAT AND GO TO THE FAMILY CENTRE FOR A CHAT AND A CUP OF TEA WITH THE STAFF." - **A LADY CLIENT OF ST. GEORGE'S CRYPT'S FAMILY CENTRE.**

NO: 88] MINCEMEAT CAKE

JULIA OLDFIELD

VOLUNTEER WORKER IN THE FAMILY CENTRE AT ST. GEORGE'S CRYPT, LEEDS

"Heavier than sponge, but lighter than fruit cake. Very moist."

INGREDIENTS

350 g (12 oz) sweet mincemeat

110 g (4 oz) brown sugar

200 g (7 oz) self-raising flour, sieved

110 g (4 oz) margarine

3 eggs

4 tablespoons milk

Oven - 170 °C, 325 F, Gas Mark 3 for 10 minutes

150 °C, 300 F, Gas Mark 2 for 1 hour

METHOD

Grease and line a 20 cm (8 inch) cake tin.

Cream the margarine and sugar together. Beat in the eggs one at a time, adding a little flour with each. Stir in the mincemeat and fold in the remaining flour. Add the milk.

Bake in a pre-heated oven at the higher temperature for 10 minutes then turn down to the lower temperature and bake for approximately 1 hour.

no: 89] PARADISE CAKE

LINDSEY PALLANT
ST. GEORGE'S CHURCH, LEEDS

INGREDIENTS

175 g (6 oz) short crust pastry (see section on handy basics)

2 round tablespoons ground almonds

2 tablespoons walnuts, chopped

75 g (3 oz) margarine

1 tablespoon jam

110 g (4 oz) sultanas

2 tablespoons glacé cherries

50 g (2 oz) caster sugar

1 egg

Oven - 180 °C, 350 F, Gas Mark 4

METHOD

Grease a 20 cm (8 inch) round tin. Line the tin with the pastry and spread with the jam.

Cream the margarine and sugar together, add the beaten eggs and the rest of the ingredients. Spread evenly over the pastry. Bake in the oven for 35-40 minutes.

SERVES 6

NO: 90] FAIL-SAFE CHOCOLATE CAKE

FIONA CASTLE
WIFE OF THE LATE ROY CASTLE

"A very versatile fail-safe chocolate cake."

INGREDIENTS

150 g (5 oz) caster sugar

2 teaspoons cocoa

1 teaspoon baking powder

150 ml (5 fl oz) milk

2 eggs

185 g (6 1/2 oz) plain flour

1 teaspoon bicarbonate of soda

2 tablespoons golden syrup

275 ml (10 fl oz) oil

Desired cake filling and topping

Oven - 170 °C, 325 F, Gas Mark 3

METHOD

Grease and line two 20 cm (8 inch) cake tins.

Place all the ingredients together in a blender and blend till just mixed (soft, runny mixture). Spread the mixture into the tins and bake for 35 minutes.

Cool and sandwich together with jam or butter cream and decorate with icing or chocolate if desired.

As an alternative, use coffee or ground almonds and grated orange or lemon rind instead of cocoa, or oatmeal, ginger and black treacle. It freezes well.

"THEY MAKE YOU FEEL SPECIAL AT THE FAMILY CENTRE."
**A LADY USER OF THE FAMILY CENTRE RUN BY
ST. GEORGE'S CRYPT.**

NO: 91 | ALL-IN-ONE CHOCOLATE SPONGE

TONY BLAIR

PRIME MINISTER OF GREAT BRITAIN & NORTHERN IRELAND

INGREDIENTS

110 g (4 oz) self-raising flour

110 g (4 oz) soft margarine or butter at room temperature

2 large eggs

1 teaspoon baking powder

110 g (4 oz) caster sugar

1 tablespoon cocoa powder

FILLING

Icing sugar

Jam and/or fresh cream

Oven - 170 °C, 325 F, Gas Mark 3

METHOD

Lightly grease and line with greaseproof paper (also greased) two 18 cm (7 inch) sponge tins and no less than 4 cm (1½ inch) deep. Take a large roomy mixing bowl and sift the flour and baking powder into it, holding the sieve high to give the flour a good airing. Then simply add all the other ingredients to the bowl, and whisk them - preferably with an electric hand whisk, until thoroughly combined. If the mixture doesn't drop off a wooden spoon easily when tapped on the side of the bowl, then add 1 or 2 teaspoons of warm tap water, and whisk again.

Now divide the mixture between the 2 prepared tins, level off and bake on the centre shelf of the oven for about 30 minutes. When cooked, leave them in the tins for about 30 seconds. Loosen the edges by sliding a palette knife all round and turn them out onto a wire cooling rack. Peel the base papers carefully and when cool, sandwich them together with the jam (or jam and fresh cream) and dust the top with icing sugar.

NO: 92] CHOCOLATE BROWNIES

JANE ASHER
ACTRESS & AUTHOR OF COOKBOOKS

"Really chocolatey, gooey brownies are delicious. You can spread them with a topping or even serve them warm with ice-cream. It's important that you use exactly the ingredients and method I have described. It's better to slightly undercook them rather than leave them in the oven too long, so that they have that lovely chewiness."

INGREDIENTS

A little oil or butter for greasing

3 eggs

1 teaspoon vanilla essence

1/4 teaspoon baking powder

25 g (1 oz) cocoa powder

110 g (4 oz) walnut pieces (optional)

200 g (7 oz) granulated sugar

5 tablespoons sunflower or vegetable oil

110 g (4 oz) plain flour

A pinch of salt

25 g (1 oz) drinking chocolate

Oven - 180 °C, 350 F, Gas Mark 4

METHOD

Pre-heat the oven. Grease and line the base of a 20 cm (8 inch) square baking tin.

Put the sugar, eggs, oil and vanilla essence into a medium-sized bowl and mix them together. Sift the flour, baking powder, salt, cocoa and drinking chocolate into another bowl. Add the flour mixture to the egg mixture and put in the walnuts if you like them. Beat it all together for 1 minute. Pour the mixture into the baking tin and smooth the top with the back of a spoon. Place in the oven and cook for about 30 minutes until just firm.

Leave to cool in the tin. When cool, turn them out of the tin and cut into 16 squares. Store in an air-tight container (unless, as in my house, they're all eaten straight away).

Variations

1. Really Chocolatey Brownies - Use 50 g (2 oz) cocoa instead of cocoa and drinking chocolate. These are very strong and dark.

2. Chocolate Chip Brownies - Stir 110 g (4 oz) plain, milk or white chocolate drops into the mixture instead of the walnuts.

3. Quick Fudge Topping - Put 225 g (8 oz) soft brown sugar, 5 tablespoons double cream, 25 g (1 oz) butter and a pinch of salt into a saucepan. Dissolve everything over a low heat, stirring, then turn up the heat and boil. Remove from the heat and allow to cool a little. Transfer to a bowl, stir in a few drops of vanilla essence and beat well until thick. Spread over the cold uncut brownies.

MAKES 16

NO: 93] LEMON POPPY SEED MUFFINS

PAULINE NELSON

MEMBER OF MUMS' GROUP OF ST. GEORGE'S CHURCH, LEEDS

INGREDIENTS

280 g (10 oz) flour

4 tablespoons poppy seeds

4 teaspoons grated lemon rind

140 g (5 oz) caster sugar

180 ml (6 fl oz) sour cream

1½ teaspoons vanilla essence

½ teaspoon salt

¼ teaspoon bicarbonate of soda

100 g (4 oz) butter or margarine

2 eggs

60 ml (2 fl oz) lemon juice

Oven - 180 °C, 350 F, Gas Mark 4

METHOD

Combine the flour, salt, poppy seeds, baking soda and lemon rind in a small bowl. In another bowl, beat the butter and sugar together until light and thick. Then beat in the eggs, one at a time. Blend in the sour cream, lemon juice and vanilla. Gradually mix in the dry ingredients.

Put the batter into muffin tins, either greased or lined with paper muffin cases. Fill each container about ¾ full. Bake for 15-20 minutes, or less if making mini-muffins.

MAKES 12-16 LARGE MUFFINS OR 30 MINI-MUFFINS

> "HELP, FRIENDSHIP, PEOPLE WHO CARE, ST. GEORGE'S CRYPT IS ALWAYS THERE.
> BARGAINS GALORE, FRIENDSHIP AND MORE. THE PLACE TO GO WHEN YOU'RE FEELING LOW."
> **A POEM BY A USER OF THE FAMILY CENTRE OF ST. GEORGE'S CRYPT**

(see photograph on p.106)

NO: 94] DES MERVELLES (JERSEY WONDERS)

JUDITH JACKSON
ST. GEORGE'S CHURCH, LEEDS

"According to Jersey folklore, wonders were cooked as the tide went out. A rising tide would mean the fat would overflow the pan! These will keep for a month."

INGREDIENTS

700 g (1½ lb) self-raising flour

110 g (4 oz) butter

1¼ litres (2 pints) cooking oil

225 g (8 oz) caster sugar

6 eggs, whisked

Extra caster sugar for sprinkling

METHOD

Sift the flour and sugar together and rub in the butter. Add the whisked eggs to make a light dough. With floured hands, make golf-sized shapes. Place on a floured baking tray and cover with a damp cloth and leave for 2 hours.

Roll out each ball into a 5 cm x 10 cm (2 inch x 4 inch) oblong. Slit the centre of each oblong and twist the top end through the slit. Pour the oil into a large pan. When the oil is hot drop 4-6 wonders in at a time (they should float) and cook for 2 minutes each side, until golden. Drain on kitchen paper and sprinkle with caster sugar.

MAKES ABOUT 40

NO: 95] YORKSHIRE MUNCH

THE MOST REVD. & RT. HON. DAVID HOPE, THE ARCHBISHOP OF YORK

"A rather modest item, and one which I remember my mother used to make for us as children but proved to be really sustaining and which I still get my sister to make when I do not have the time, particularly if I am going off on a trek to Scotland."

INGREDIENTS

150 g (5 oz) margarine

2 tablespoons golden syrup

50 g (2 oz) sugar

175 g (6 oz) quaker oats

Oven - 180 °C, 350 F, Gas Mark 4

METHOD

Grease an 18 cm (7 inch) square tin.

Cream the margarine and the sugar together. Warm the golden syrup and add to the creamed mixture. Stir in the quaker oats.

Press into the tin and bake in a moderate oven for 30-45 minutes until golden brown.

Allow to cool in the tin, then slice into squares.

MAKES ABOUT 12

NO: 96] CRUNCHIE OAT COOKIES

DEBBIE WHITEHEAD
ST. GEORGE'S CHURCH, LEEDS

INGREDIENTS

175 g (6 oz) porridge oats

110 g (4 oz) margarine

2 level tablespoons golden syrup

110 g (4 oz) cherries, chopped

110 g (4 oz) plain flour

110 g (4 oz) soft light brown sugar

1 level teaspoon bicarbonate of soda

Oven - 180 °C, 350 F, Gas Mark 4

METHOD

Liberally grease 2 or 3 large baking sheets.

Mix together the oats, flour and cherries. Melt the margarine in a pan with the sugar and syrup. Remove from the heat and immediately add the bicarbonate of soda to the pan mixture and stir. Mix all the ingredients together and shape into walnut-sized balls.

Space well apart on the baking sheets (as they will spread during cooking) and gently press down to flatten the tops. Bake for 10-15 minutes, or until lightly browned. Let the cookies cool slightly before removing them from the baking sheet (2 minutes). Place on a wire rack to cool completely.

MAKES ABOUT 20

> "YOU'RE ALWAYS WELCOME. THERE'S ALWAYS SOMEONE TO TALK TO"
> **A WOMAN CLIENT OF ST. GEORGE'S CRYPT'S FAMILY CENTRE**

(see photograph on p.106)

NO: 97] GYPSY DREAMS

ANNE DENT

ST. GEORGE'S CHURCH, LEEDS

INGREDIENTS

100 g (4 oz) self-raising flour

75 g (3 oz) oats

1 dessertspoon cocoa

100 g (4 oz) margarine

50 g (2 oz) caster sugar

1 teaspoon golden syrup dissolved in 2 tablespoons hot water

FILLING

25 g (1 oz) margarine

50 g (2 oz) icing sugar

$^{1}/_{2}$ teaspoon cocoa

Oven - 180 ℃, 350 F, Gas Mark 4

METHOD

Lightly grease 2 baking trays.

Cream the margarine and sugar together. Add the dry ingredients alternately with the syrup and water. Take approximately 1 rounded teaspoonful of the mixture and roll into a ball. Place on the baking trays and bake in the oven for 15-20 minutes. The mixture will spread slightly while cooking.

To make the filling, mix together the margarine, cocoa and icing sugar, and use to sandwich the biscuits together.

MAKES ABOUT 12

NO: 98] PEANUT BUTTER COOKIES

MARY BURDON

MISSION PARTNER OF ST. GEORGE'S CHURCH, LEEDS, WORKING IN AFRICA

*"Peanuts are one of the staple foods in the Democratic Republic of Congo.
We grow them in our garden and these biscuits are a favourite with
all the family."*

INGREDIENTS

110 g (4 oz) margarine

225 g (8 oz) sugar

275 g (10 oz) plain flour

1/4 teaspoon bicarbonate of soda

110 g (4 oz) peanut butter

1 egg

1/2 teaspoon baking powder

1/4 teaspoon salt

Oven - 170 °C, 325 F, Gas Mark 3

METHOD

Grease 2 baking trays. Sift the flour and mix all the ingredients together to form a stiff paste. Leave this in the refrigerator for 30 minutes.

Make small round balls out of the mixture and place on the baking trays. Press gently with a fork and bake for 15 minutes.

MAKES ABOUT 24

NO: 99] WELSH CAKES

NEIL KINNOCK

TRANSPORT COMMISSIONER, EUROPEAN UNION 1998

INGREDIENTS

225 g (8 oz) self-raising flour

75 g (3 oz) currants

1 egg

110 g (4 oz) butter or margarine

75 g (3 oz) caster sugar

Oil for cooking

METHOD

Rub the butter into the flour. When the mixture resembles breadcrumbs add the currants and the sugar. Beat the egg and add it to the mixture. Use your hands to make a dough and add a little milk if it is too dry.

Now roll the dough out on a floured working surface. Roll it out to about 5 mm (1/4 inch) thick and cut into rounds with a 6½ cm (2½ inch) cutter.

Brush a griddle pan with the oil and place over a medium heat, cook the cakes for about 2-3 minutes on each side. Make sure they are cooked through and a good golden brown colour.

Serve them as they are, or buttered with good Welsh honey.

MAKES ABOUT 20

"COMING TO THE FAMILY CENTRE AT ST. GEORGE'S CRYPT HAS HELPED ME TO GET BACK ON MY FEET AFTER A BAD TIME."
A GRATEFUL USER OF THE FAMILY CENTRE.

NO: 100] YOGHURT SCONES

LIZ McCOLGAN
WOMEN'S 10,000M WORLD CHAMPION (1991) & WINNER OF THE LONDON MARATHON (1996)

INGREDIENTS

225 g (8 oz) wholemeal flour-
-(alternatively use half wholemeal and half plain white flour)

1/2 teaspoon baking powder

1 tablespoon muscovado sugar

Milk for brushing

Sesame seeds for sprinkling (optional)

1/2 teaspoon salt

50 g (2 oz) margarine

150 g (5 oz) natural low fat yoghurt

25 g (1 oz) raisins

Oven - 220 °C, 425 F, Gas Mark 7

METHOD

Pre-heat the oven.

Mix the flour and salt together and sift in the baking powder. Rub in the margarine until the mixture resembles bread crumbs. Stir in the sugar. Add the raisins and the yoghurt and mix into a dough. Turn onto a floured surface, knead lightly and roll out to 2 cm (3/4 inch) thickness. Cut into 5 cm (2 inch) rounds with a cutter.

Place on a floured baking tray and brush with milk. If desired, sprinkle with sesame seeds (optional). Bake in the oven for 12-15 minutes. Cool on a wire rack.

MAKES 12-14

NO: 101 | PHIL'S BREAD

ANGELA WRIGHT

MEMBER OF MUMS' GROUP OF ST. GEORGE'S CHURCH, LEEDS

"My husband Phil makes this faithfully every week. The quantities could be halved, but it's easier to measure like this."

INGREDIENTS

1 bag (1¹/2 kg, 3¹/4 lb) strong white flour

3 dessertspoons dried active yeast

6 dessertspoons sunflower oil

1 bag (1¹/2 kg, 3¹/4 lb) strong brown flour

2 dessertspoons salt

1³/4 litres (3 pints) warm water

5-6 dessertspoons of a mixture of any of sunflower, sesame, millet, poppy seeds, cracked or kibbled wheat and buckwheat

Oven - 220 °C, 425 F, Gas Mark 7

METHOD

Grease 6 loaf tins.

Place the flour, yeast, salt and 'bits' in a bowl. Stir and make a well in the centre. Measure in the oil, then the water. Mix and knead for a good 5-10 minutes, until the dough is smooth and elastic. Cover with a tea towel and leave to rise in the bowl until it doubles in size.

Punch down and remove from the bowl. Divide into six, knead and form into loaves. Place in the loaf tins, cover and again leave until double in size. Bake for 30 minutes on low and middle shelves of the oven. When the time is up, swap the loaves from upper to lower shelves, removing the tins from the top loaves and turning the bread upside down onto the lower shelf. Leave for a further 10 minutes. Remove the lower loaves, turn the upper loaves upside down as before, removing the tins. Bake for 10 more minutes.

The bread is cooked if the bottom sounds hollow when tapped. Cool on racks. This bread freezes well.

MAKES 6 LOAVES

NO: 102] SEVILLE MARMALADE

CHRISTINE HILL
MEMBER OF MUMS' GROUP OF ST. GEORGE'S CHURCH, LEEDS

INGREDIENTS

1.3 kg (3 lb) frozen Seville oranges

4 tablespoons lemon juice

1³/4 litres (3 pints) water

2.6 kg (6 lb) granulated sugar, warmed

METHOD

Place the frozen oranges (do not thaw) and water into a pressure cooker, cover and bring to 15 lb pressure for 20 minutes. Cool the pan and release the lid. Test the oranges for tenderness by pricking with a cocktail stick.

Lift all the fruit out into a colander (catch any juice in a bowl underneath and return to the pan). Cut the oranges in half, remove all pips and put pips back into the pan, cover and bring to 15 lb pressure for a further 5 minutes.

Meanwhile, slice all the orange peel (or use a food processor). Put this peel, lemon juice and warm sugar into a preserving pan. Add the strained water and juice from the pressure cooker and throw away the pips. Stir over the heat to dissolve the sugar then boil rapidly.

Test for setting after about 10 minutes by putting a small amount onto a saucer and letting it cool. When cool, the skin that forms should wrinkle when pushed with a finger.

Pour into hot clean jars, cover and label.

MAKES ABOUT 10 JARS

"THE STAFF OF ST. GEORGE'S CRYPT'S FAMILY CENTRE HAVE TIME FOR YOU. YOU'RE LISTENED TO."
A SATISFIED USER OF THE FAMILY CENTRE RUN BY ST. GEORGE'S CRYPT.

NO: 103] BLACKBERRY & APPLE JAM

MOLLY ROWLAND
SUPPORTER OF ST. GEORGE'S CRYPT, LEEDS

INGREDIENTS

2.2 kg (5 lb) blackberries

425 ml (3/4 pint) water

450 g (1 lb) Bramley apples

2.6 kg (6 lb) sugar

METHOD

Wash the fruit and peel and core the apples. Boil the fruit and water gently for 40-45 minutes, stirring occasionally. Add the sugar and boil rapidly for 10-15 minutes. Test for setting by putting a teaspoon of the jam on a cold saucer. Once the jam is cooled it should wrinkle when touched.

Stand the pan in cold water and stir rapidly until any scum disappears. Pour into clean warm jam jars and seal. This jam will keep indefinitely.

MAKES ABOUT 12 JARS

Strawberry Jam - As an alternative, to make strawberry jam use 2.2 kg (5 lb) strawberries, 450 g (1 lb) gooseberries, 2.6 kg (6 lb) sugar and the juice of 1 lemon. Follow the method as above but do NOT add any water or it will not set.

NO: 104] LEMON CURD

RUTH COGGAN
MISSION PARTNER OF ST. GEORGE'S CHURCH, LEEDS, WORKING IN PAKISTAN

"I use 5 little 'nimbus' in Pakistan instead of the one big lemon."

INGREDIENTS

1 egg, beaten

75 g (3 oz) granulated sugar

25 g (1 oz) butter

Juice and finely grated rind of one large lemon

METHOD

Place all the ingredients in a clean jam jar. Stand the jar in a saucepan of water to come half way up the jar. Simmer gently, stirring occasionally, until it thickens. Remove the jar from the pan and when cold cover with a lid or cling film. Keep in the refrigerator and use within a week.

MAKES 1 JAR

NO: 105] SUGAR-FREE-VEGETARIAN MINCEMEAT

INGREDIENTS

150 g (5 oz) currants, chopped

150 g (5 oz) sultanas, chopped

1 eating apple, grated including the skin

Grated rind of 1 large orange

1-2 teaspoons mixed spice

1 tablespoon of spirit, e.g. sherry or brandy (optional)

150 g (5 oz) raisins, chopped

50 g (2 oz) ground almonds

110 g (4 oz) carrot, finely grated

1-2 teaspoons orange juice to moisten

1-2 teaspoons nutmeg

METHOD

Mix all the ingredients together well. Place in clean jam jars and seal.

MAKES 2 JARS

"I FEEL MUCH BETTER NOW I'M HERE IN THIS HOSTEL.
I'M GETTING SORTED AND THE STAFF ARE HELPING ME."
**A RESIDENT OF ST GEORGE'S CRYPT'S HOSTEL
FOR YOUNG HOMELESS MEN AND WOMEN.**

A Grace

For food, for shelter, for the love of friends and family
we thank you, God.
for a heart that will share these gifts with others,
we ask you, God.

Amen.

SNACKS
WITH A SMILE

NO: 106] BEST SANDWICH EVER

VICTORIA WOOD
COMEDIENNE

METHOD

Two big slices of wholemeal bread, preferably with bits in. Bits of butter to spread on them.

Lots of avocado, tomato, cucumber and cress. (Alfalfa sprouts too if you live in one of the three places that sell them!)

Put it all together. (PUT THE BREAD ON THE OUTSIDE.)

Put real mayonnaise and salt and pepper in the middle.

EAT IT!

NO: 107] COCKLES

JULIE WALTERS
COMMEDIENNE & ACTRESS

INGREDIENTS

150 ml (¼ pint) fresh cockles   2 slices wholemeal bread

Butter   Freshly ground pepper

METHOD

Butter the bread. Place the cockles on one piece and sprinkle with pepper. Cover with the other piece. Open mouth, shove in, clamp teeth down on bread and masticate - OK?

NO: 108] TOAST

CLIVE ANDERSON
BBC TV & RADIO PRESENTER

METHOD

Cut 2 slices of bread from a loaf of your choice. (Quick method: take 2 pieces from a sliced loaf.) Put under a grill or into a toaster and toast for 2 or 3 minutes, or until golden brown on both sides. Spread with butter or vegetable oil-based substitute. Then spread with jam or (my favourite) marmalade. Serve on a plate with a cup of tea.

NO: 109] CHEESE & ONION ON TOAST

JOHN HUMPHRYS
BBC TV NEWSREADER & PRESENTER OF BBC RADIO 4'S 'TODAY' PROGRAMME

"One of the abiding smells of my childhood is cheese being grilled on a tin plate for tea on winter Saturday afternoons. It always brings back the sound of the sports announcer reading the football results on the Home Service. I loved toasted cheese then and I love it to this day."

INGREDIENTS

Bread
Cheese
Thickly sliced onion

METHOD

Toast one side of some good bread, preferably soda bread from my local baker, and slice a little cheese on the other side and toast that too. Then when the cheese is soft, put thick slices of onion on the cheese and add another layer of cheese. Then grill again to melt the top layer of cheese. Wonderful. Even better if the cheese is organic farmhouse cheddar.

NO: 110] GARLIC CHEESE

DIANE COWLES
MISSION PARTNER OF ST. GEORGE'S CHURCH, LEEDS

"This is served in Russia with fresh bread and crackers as part of the salad course, but would do well served following a meal as part of the cheese board."

INGREDIENTS

3 medium garlic cloves
225 g (8 oz) cheddar or other hard cheese
5 level tablespoons mayonnaise

METHOD

Grate the cheese very finely into a bowl, crush and add the garlic. Add the mayonnaise and mix together well. Serve with crackers or fresh bread.

MAKES 300 g (10 oz)

NO: 111] LEEK, EGG & CHEESE PUFFS

NICK PARK
CREATOR OF WALLACE & GROMIT

INGREDIENTS

225 g (8 oz) leeks, washed and sliced

1 teaspoon vegetable oil

Fresh ground black pepper

75 g (3 oz) Wensleydale cheese, cut into cubes

4 x 10 cm (4 inch) squares of puff pastry, thawed

Salt, to taste

1 small onion, peeled and sliced

1/2 teaspoon coriander seeds, crushed

2 hard boiled eggs, shelled and halved, lengthways

Beaten egg to glaze

Oven - 220 °C, 425 F, Gas Mark 7

METHOD

Cook the leeks in boiling salted water for 3 minutes, or until just tender. Drain and allow to cool. Heat the oil in a small pan and sauté the onion until lightly browned. Add the salt, pepper, coriander seeds and leeks. Cook for a further minute. Allow to cool for 10 minutes and then stir in the cheese.

Brush the edges of the pastry squares with the beaten egg. Divide the filling evenly between the squares, placing it just off-centre, and top each half with a boiled egg. Fold the pastry over to make a triangle. Seal the edges firmly and brush the tops with beaten egg.

Bake in the oven for 15-20 minutes, until puffed up and golden brown. Serve hot with a crisp green salad, or leave to cool to make a good picnic or packed lunch dish.

MAKES 4

NO: 112] DOCK PUDDING

SIR BERNARD INGHAM

FORMER PRESS SECRETARY TO PRIME MINISTER MARGARET THATCHER
AND PATRON OF THE 'MORE THAN A ROOF' APPEAL

"Herewith my favourite recipe. It is for a spring (March-April) dish, local to my native Hebden Bridge, but it apparently has its equivalent in North West Cumbria. It is widely assumed to have cleansed the blood of locals in days of yore after a stodgy winter diet. Lord Haw Haw, the traitor, used it in his wartime broadcasts as evidence of starvation in the North of England because, he said, the people were eating "grass" At that very time, I used to collect dock leaves at a tanner (six old pence) per carrier bag for sale to housewives. There are now the International Dock Pudding Championships held in May in Mytholmroyd, the next village to Hebden Bridge."

INGREDIENTS

900 g (2 lb) fresh young leaves of the sweet dock (*polygonum bistorta*, **NOT** the cow dock)

225 g (8 oz) nettles

1/2 a teacupful of oatmeal (or as required by taste)

Salt and pepper

2 large onions

A knob of butter

METHOD

Wash and de-stalk the dock leaves and nettles. Place in a pan. Chop the onions into small pieces and add to the docks and nettles. Add the seasoning and boil until the greens are tender. Add the oatmeal and boil for 20 minutes, stirring to avoid lumps. Strain and store in jam jars

NO: 113] BAKED BEANS ON TOAST

ROWAN ATKINSON

COMEDIAN

METHOD

Heat the beans in a pan until they go all bubbly. Pour over toast and serve.

NO: 114] CHIP BUTTIE

TERRY WOGAN
BBC TV & RADIO PRESENTER

"There is nothing like a chip buttie to bring back memories of one's boyhood days. It's not an expensive, fancy dish - anyone can make it - and the taste is great."

METHOD

Take two thick slices of crusty white bread. Spread both slices liberally with plenty of butter. Fill with sizzling hot, freshly fried chips. Salt and vinegar to taste.

EAT IMMEDIATELY

NO: 115] BACHELOR SCRAMBLED EGGS & TOMATOES

ROLF HARRIS
ARTIST & TV PERSONALITY

INGREDIENTS

2 eggs per person	2 tomatoes per person
Spring onion, finely chopped (optional)	Milk
Butter	Salt and pepper

METHOD

Melt a small splodge of butter in a frying pan and drop in the spring onion. Cook over a slow heat for a short while. Then add a slosh of milk, but not too much or the eggs will be watery later. Remove from the heat and break the eggs into the pan. Add a dusting of salt to each egg and as much pepper as you enjoy.

Return to the low heat and graunch up the eggs with a wooden spoon and generally scramble them around. The heat must be low - nothing is worse than little black horribly tasting burnt bits in scrambled egg.

Meanwhile, cut your tomato in half and place under the grill. Put the flat side down first and grill until the skin shrivels up and starts to go black. Then turn over, add a dusting of salt and grill the flat side.

Your scrambled egg should be just starting to solidify, so take it off the heat for a tick while you pop in your two beautifully grilled tomatoes. The skin on the smooth side just comes away but you will need to cut out the core of the tomato.

Return to the heat while you squelch up the tomato into bite sized pieces with the wooden spoon.
Don't dry it up too much. DELICIOUS!

NO: 116] CORNFLAKES

JOHN CLEESE
COMEDIAN & ACTOR

"Its very simple to make and absolutely delicious."

METHOD

Buy a packet of cornflakes.
Open the cardboard box.
Open the sort of plastic packet inside the box.
Pour some of the contents (sort of yellowy brownish bits of things) on to a plate.
Buy a bottle of milk.
Take the top off the thin end of the bottle.
Invert the bottle gently over the cornflakes making sure that the milk does not go over the edge of the plate.

An alternative is to use Coca Cola instead of milk. Add basil as required.

NO: 117] SINGLE MAN'S LUNCH

SIR JIMMY SAVILE
TV PRESENTER, PERSONALITY & 'FIX-IT' MAN!

Jimmy has no cookers in any of his flats so something swift and simple is the order of the day!

INGREDIENTS

1 tin soup
1 tin beans

METHOD

Pour soup into dish.
Pour beans into same dish.
Stir together.
Put in microwave.
Heat and eat.

SERVES 1

A FEW HANDY
BASICS

NO: 118   SHORTCRUST PASTRY

NO: 119   PUFF PASTRY

NO: 118] SHORTCRUST PASTRY

SHORTCRUST PASTRY

150 g (6 oz) pastry = 100 g (4 oz) flour and 50 g (2 oz) fat (see note below)

250 g (9 oz) pastry = 175 g (6 oz) flour and 75 g (3 oz) fat

350 g (12 oz) pastry = 225 g (8 oz) flour and 110 g (4 oz) fat

450 g (1 lb) pastry = 300 g (11 oz) flour and 150 g (5 oz) fat

A pinch of salt

Cold water to bind

Sift the flour and salt into a large bowl. Cut the fat into small pieces and add to the flour. Rub the fat in with your fingertips until the mixture resembles fine breadcrumbs. Add a little cold water and mix with a palette knife until the mixture begins to stick together in large lumps. Bring the mixture together with your hands to form a smooth ball of dough. Wrap in cling film and chill in the refrigerator for about 30 minutes before rolling out.

Note : The fat can be all butter, all margarine, all lard, or half butter or margarine and half lard depending on personal preference.

NO: 119] PUFF PASTRY

PUFF PASTRY

100 g (4 oz) pastry = 50 g (2 oz) flour and 50 g (2 oz) butter or margarine

400 g (14 oz) pastry = 200 g (7 oz) flour and 200 g (7 oz) butter or margarine

450 g (1 lb) pastry = 225 g (8 oz) flour and 225 g (8 oz) butter or margarine

A pinch of salt

Chilled water to bind

A dash of lemon juice

Sift the flour and salt into a bowl. Cut 25 g (1 oz) of the butter into small pieces, add to the flour and rub in. Using a palette knife, stir in enough water and lemon juice to make a soft elastic dough.

Roll out to a neat oblong shape. Place the remaining butter in the centre of the dough. Fold one-third of the pastry over the butter, followed by the other third to give a neat shape. Turn the dough at right-angles, seal the ends and then, using a rolling pin, rib the pastry dough at regular intervals. This is the first folding. Continue like this, giving the pastry a total of six rollings and foldings. Chill well between rollings. Shape the pastry as required, then place in the refrigerator for 30 minutes before baking as in the recipe.

CHEFS MENUS
For
SPECIAL OCCASIONS

NO: 120 VALENTINE'S DAY MENU (STEVE CHESNUTT)

Warm Salad of Smoked Salmon with Asparagus

Roast Breast of Chicken with Wild Mushrooms & Parma Ham
on a Risotto of Fine Herbs

Tarte Tatin of Apple & Apricot with a Plum & Cinnamon Custard

NO: 121 WINTER MENU (ANTON EDELMAN)

Tiger Prawns in Filo Pastry with Mango Sauce

The Savoy's Chicken Pie served with Olive Oil Potatoes

Hot Chocolate Pudding with Mint Custard Sauce

NO: 122 SPRING MENU (MIKE PICKEN)

Medallion of Salmon on Sweet Potato Mash with Mustard Sauce

Lamb Hotpot with Fennel & Dill Soda Scones

Whisky & Honey Base with Ginger Berries

NO: 123 SUMMER MENU (RAYMOND BLANC)

Grilled Summer Vegetables

Best End of Lamb with a Herb Crust

Poached White Peaches with Orange Sabayon & Wild Strawberries

NO: 124 AUTUMN MENU (MICHEL FLAMME)

Roasted Scallops with a Compôte of Onion & Chives & Belgian Endive

Cutlet of Pork with Artichoke & Olive, Bay Leaf Jus

Caramelised John O' Gold

NO: 125 WINTER SUPPER (LINDA McCARTNEY)

Pasta & Bean Salad with Basil & Pecorino

Winter Lasagne

Floating Islands

NO: 120] VALENTINE'S DAY MENU (SERVES TWO)

STEVE CHESNUTT

EXECUTIVE HEAD CHEF, BOAR'S HEAD RESTAURANT, RIPLEY CASTLE, YORKSHIRE

The Boar's Head is an 18th century coaching inn within an estate village.

WARM SALAD OF SMOKED SALMON WITH ASPARAGUS

INGREDIENTS

6 slices of smoked salmon

12 tips of asparagus

40 ml olive oil

Fresh herbs - dill and chervil

A selection of salad leaves

10 ml lemon juice

Salt & pepper

METHOD

Form the sliced salmon into a rosette shape by wrapping it round while twisting it at the same time. Place onto a small baking sheet. Whilst this is placed under the grill to cook gently, you can arrange the salad on the plate and prepare the dressing.

Place the cooked asparagus around the salad leaves. The middle part of the asparagus can be sliced very finely and added to the dressing raw. Once the salmon is lightly grilled, arrange around the salad alternately with the asparagus tips. Season and garnish with sprigs of fresh herbs.

(see photograph on p.107)

ROAST BREAST OF CHICKEN WITH WILD MUSHROOM & PARMA HAM ON A RISOTTO OF FINE HERBS

INGREDIENTS

2 chicken breasts - skinless and boneless

125 g (4¹/2 oz) Arborio rice

1 small shallot

50 ml (2 fl oz) gravy (red wine sauce)

10 g (¹/2 oz) butter

100 g (4 oz) mixed wild mushrooms

500 ml (17 fl oz) chicken stock

2 slices of Parma ham (or similar)

Herbs - parsley, chives and tarragon

Oven - 180 °C, 350 F, Gas Mark 4

METHOD

Sauté the mushrooms in butter. Cut a pocket in the chicken breast and fill with the mushrooms and season with salt and pepper. Wrap a slice of the Parma ham around the chicken breast and roast in a moderate oven for 20 minutes.

To make the risotto, first sauté the finely chopped shallots for a few minutes and then add the rice. Sauté again for a few minutes then little by little add the chicken stock, continuously stirring. This will take about 15-20 minutes to cook. Add the chopped herbs to the risotto and check the seasoning. Press the risotto into a circular cutter. Cut the chicken in half and press this on top of the risotto and pour the gravy around the outside. Garnish with some of the fresh herbs.

TARTE TATIN OF APPLE & APRICOT WITH PLUM & CINAMMON CUSTARD

INGREDIENTS

Pre-made puff pastry (to make your own see section on handy basics)

2 fresh green apples (eaters not cookers)

5 g butter

A little ground cinnamon

275 ml (10 fl oz) double cream

10 dried apricots, soaked in brandy

10 g (½ oz) brown sugar

2 plums

4 egg yolks

1 fresh vanilla pod or 4 drops of essence

Oven - 200 °C, 400 F, Gas Mark 6

METHOD

To make the custard, boil the cream with the vanilla pods and pour onto the yolks, whisking continuously.

To make the tart, cut a disk of puff pastry the size of your mould. Sugar and butter the mould and place the apricots in the bottom. Then layer the slices of apple above the height of the mould (they will cook down for a good layer of cooked apple). Place the disk of puff pastry on top of this and then bake in the oven for approximately 10-15 minutes, or until golden brown. Turn out when cooked so that the pastry is on the bottom. Finish the custard with small chopped fresh plums and a little ground cinnamon. Garnish with fresh mint leaves.

Heart-shaped designs can be added to the plate for a Valentine's menu.

NO: 121] WINTER MENU (SERVES FOUR)

ANTON EDELMANN

EXECUTIVE HEAD CHEF, THE SAVOY HOTEL, LONDON

TIGER PRAWNS IN FILO PASTRY

INGREDIENTS

16 raw tiger prawns

16 squares of filo pastry dough, each 10 cm x 10 cm (4 inch x 4 inch)

1 egg yolk

4 handfuls of mixed salad leaves, weighing about 90 g (3 oz)

Mango Sauce

1 large ripe mango

4 tablespoons mayonnaise (see page 154)

Sea salt and freshly ground black pepper

32 large fresh basil leaves

Vegetable oil for deep frying

4 tablespoons soy vinaigrette (see page 154)

1 hard-boiled egg yolk

2 teaspoons finely shredded fresh basil

METHOD

First make the mango sauce. Peel the mango and cut the flesh from the flat central stone. Chop the flesh coarsely. You should have about 100 g (3½ oz) of mango flesh. Put the flesh into a food processor or blender with the hard-boiled egg yolk and mayonnaise and work until smooth. Press the mixture through a fine sieve into a bowl. Stir in the basil and season with salt and pepper to taste. Set the sauce aside.

Peel the prawns, make a shallow cut down the rounded back of each and remove the dark intestinal vein. Rinse the prawns and pat dry with paper towels. Season with salt and pepper.

Work with one filo square at a time and keep the rest covered with cling film.

Put a filo square on the work surface and brush it with melted butter. Set a basil leaf in the centre and put a prawn on top. Lightly beat the egg yolk and brush a little on the edges of the filo square. Fold 2 opposite sides of the square over the prawn and press to seal. Press the ends together to seal. Wrap and seal the remaining prawns in the same way.

Heat a pan of oil to 165-175 °C, 330-345 F.

Meanwhile, wash and dry the salad leaves thoroughly.

When the oil is hot, add the prawns in filo, 4 at a time. Fry for 3 minutes or until golden and crisp, turning them over a few times so that they brown evenly. Drain on paper towels. At the end of frying, turn up the heat under the pan until the oil is 180 °C, 350 F. Add the remaining basil leaves and fry for a few seconds until crisp, bright green and translucent; drain.

Toss the salad leaves in the soy vinaigrette and divide among the plates piling the leaves in a mound at the top. Arrange the prawns in filo in the centre of the plates and garnish with the fried basil. Serve with the mango sauce.

SOY VINAIGRETTE

INGREDIENTS

100 ml (3¹/₂ fl oz) orange juice

1 tablespoon soy sauce

Freshly ground black pepper

1 tablespoon white wine vinegar

4 tablespoons olive oil

METHOD

Put the orange juice in a small pan and boil until reduced to 1 tablespoon. Set aside to cool completely.

Combine all the ingredients in a bowl and whisk well to mix.

MAYONNAISE

INGREDIENTS

2 egg yolks

2 teaspoons Dijon mustard

Salt and freshly ground white pepper

2 tablespoons white wine vinegar

A few drops Worcestershire sauce

500 ml (16 fl oz) vegetable oil

METHOD

Combine the egg yolks, vinegar, mustard and Worcestershire sauce in a food processor. Season with salt and pepper. Mix together until smoothly blended. With the machine running, add the oil slowly through the feed tube. Start with a few drops, then increase to a thin stream.

When all the oil has been incorporated and the mayonnaise is thick, taste it and add more mustard, vinegar, salt and pepper as required.

THE SAVOY'S CHICKEN PIE

"This simple yet delicious dish brings out the deep, rich flavour of chicken. It is ideal for entertaining because there is very little to do at the end."

INGREDIENTS

2 chickens, each weighing about 1 kg (2¹/4 lb)
200 g (7 oz) button mushrooms
Salt and freshly ground black pepper
1 tablespoon chopped mixed fresh tarragon and parsley
2 hard-boiled eggs
1 egg yolk

2 onions, finely chopped
45 g (1¹/2 oz) unsalted butter
500 ml (16 fl oz) chicken essence *(see page 156)*
4 slices of back bacon
400 g (14 oz) puff pastry
(to make this yourself see section on handy basics)

Oven - 190 °C, 375 F, Gas Mark 5

METHOD

Cut the legs off the chickens and shape them into neat 'butterflies' *. Also, remove the wingtips and wishbone and take the breasts off. Peel and finely chop the onions. Trim and quarter the mushrooms. Melt the butter in a saucepan over a low heat and cook the onions until soft and translucent, stirring often. Add the mushrooms and season. Cook for another minute, stirring.

Season the chicken legs and add them to the pan. Pour in the chicken essence. Bring to the boil, then reduce the heat and simmer for about 20 minutes. Add the chicken breasts and continue simmering for 10 minutes.

Remove the chicken from the pan and set aside to cool. Increase the heat and boil the cooking liquid for about 10 minutes or until it has reduced by about one-third. Remove from the heat and season. Allow to cool, then stir in the herbs.

Remove any rind from the bacon, then wrap the chicken breasts in the bacon slices. Shell the hard-boiled eggs and cut them in half. Arrange the chicken breasts and legs and egg halves in a deep 1³/4 litre (3 pint) pie dish or baking dish. Taste the cooking liquid for seasoning, then pour it into the dish.

Roll out the puff pastry dough into an oval or round (according to the shape of the pie dish) that is 8¹/2 cm (3¹/2 inches) larger than the top of the dish. Lay the dough over the pie dish, leaving the dough to hang evenly over the edges. Lightly beat the egg yolk with 1 teaspoon of water and brush this egg wash over the pastry dough. Allow it to dry, then brush the dough with egg wash again. Leave to rest in a cool place for 15 minutes.

Heat the oven. Bake the pie for 40 minutes or until the pastry is risen and golden brown.

* *To shape a chicken leg 'butterfly' - If there is a knuckle bone, twist it off. Cut through the skin around the leg bone about 4 cm (1¹/2 inches) from the end of the drumstick, then remove the skin to expose the bone at the end of the drumstick. Make a lengthwise cut in the thigh, to the bone, and cut around the ball and socket joint between the thigh and drumstick. Nearly cut out the thigh bone and the joint. Make an incision in the far end of the thigh meat and push the exposed end of the drumstick bone through it.*

CHICKEN ESSENCE

INGREDIENTS

2 chickens, each weighing about 1.2 kg (2³/4 lb)	2 onions
2 carrots	2 celery stalks
1 teaspoon black peppercorns	1 bay leaf
2 sprigs of fresh thyme	A few parsley stalks
Salt	

METHOD

Cut off the chicken breasts and reserve them for another dish. Pull off as much of the skin from the chickens as possible and discard it. Chop the chicken carcasses, wings and leg portions into pieces and put them in a stock pot or large saucepan. Cover with 3¹/2 litres (6 pints) cold water and bring slowly to simmering point, skimming often to remove all the froth that rises. Simmer for 10 minutes.

Peel or trim the vegetables and chop them coarsely. Crush the peppercorns coarsely with the base of a small heavy saucepan. Add the vegetables, herbs, peppercorns and a little salt to the pan. Continue simmering very gently for 1 hour. Turn up the heat a little so the liquid is simmering a little more quickly, but not boiling. Simmer for a further hour. Strain the essence and allow to cool completely. Remove any fat from the surface before using.

OLIVE OIL POTATOES

INGREDIENTS

700 g (1¹/2 lb) potatoes	150 ml (¹/4 pint) olive oil, preferably extra virgin
45 g (1¹/2 oz) garlic cloves (about 18 medium-sized)	Salt and freshly ground black pepper to taste
4 tablespoons milk	5 tablespoons double cream

METHOD

Peel the potatoes and cut into large cubes. Place in a saucepan. Just cover with cold water and add one-third of the oil, the peeled garlic cloves and salt. Bring to the boil and simmer for 15-20 minutes or until the potatoes are tender but not mushy. Drain well. Transfer the garlic to a board and crush with the side of a knife. Heat 1 tablespoon of olive oil in a frying pan over a moderately low heat and cook the garlic for 1 minute. Do not allow it to colour. Return the garlic to the potatoes and press through a fine sieve into a bowl, or use a potato ricer or masher. Heat the milk, cream and remaining oil in a saucepan, gradually add to the potatoes, mixing well with a wooden spoon. Season with salt and pepper and serve.

HOT CHOCOLATE PUDDING

INGREDIENTS

150 g (5 oz) good quality plain chocolate

3 eggs

Soft unsalted butter to grease the dishes

Mint Custard Sauce (see below)

15 g (1/2 oz) unsalted butter

3 tablespoons caster sugar

Icing sugar to finish

Oven - 220 °C, 425 F, Gas mark 7

METHOD

Melt the chocolate with the butter in a heavy-based saucepan over a very low heat. Remove the mixture from the heat and pour into a bowl. Separate the eggs, taking care not to have any trace of yolk in the whites. Beat the egg yolks into the melted chocolate.

In a large clean bowl, whisk the egg whites with the caster sugar to a stiff peak. Stir a spoonful of the whites into the chocolate mixture to loosen it, then fold in the remaining whites with a metal spoon. Cover and refrigerate for 11/2-2 hours.

Generously butter the insides of four 81/2 cm (31/4 inch) diameter ramekins and spoon the chocolate mixture in (it should come 5 mm (1/4 inch) from the top). Bake for 15 minutes, or until risen. Remove from the oven and set aside in a warm place to rest for 15 minutes.

Loosen the sides of each pudding with a small sharp knife, then turn it out into your hand. Set the pudding right side up in the centre of a warm plate. Dust lightly with icing sugar and serve, with the mint custard sauce.

MINT CUSTARD SAUCE

INGREDIENTS

400 ml (14 fl oz) milk

7 egg yolks

2 tablespoons fresh mint, very finely chopped

1 vanilla pod

80 g (21/2 oz) caster sugar

METHOD

Put the milk in a heavy-based saucepan. Split the vanilla pod open and add to the pan. Heat until bubbles form around the edge. Remove from the heat and set aside in a warm place to infuse for 10 minutes. Meanwhile whisk the egg yolks with the sugar in a bowl set over a pan of hot water until the sugar has dissolved and the mixture is pale, thick and increased in volume. Incorporate half the warm milk, whisking well. Heat the milk remaining in the pan to just below a simmer. Gradually add the milk and egg yolk mixture in a steady stream, stirring constantly with a wooden spoon. Cook over a low heat, stirring until the sauce thickens enough to coat the back of a spoon thinly. Strain the sauce through a fine sieve into a bowl. Add the mint and stir in. Set the bowl in a container of iced water to prevent the sauce from cooking further. Leave to cool.

NO: 122] SPRING MENU (SERVES FOUR)

MIKE PICKEN

EXECUTIVE CHEF, GLENEAGLES HOTEL, SCOTLAND

"I am honoured to be asked to present a recipe for such a deserving charity."

MEDALLION OF SALMON ON SWEET POTATO MASH WITH MUSTARD SAUCE

INGREDIENTS

4 salmon medallion pieces (each: 50g/2 oz)

75g (3 oz) shallots, chopped

32 sugar snap peas

1 teaspoon Arran mustard

1/4 bunch spring onions

1 dessertspoon créme fraiche

Salt and pepper

175g (6 oz) sweet potato

10g (1/2 oz) chives, chopped

170 ml (6 fl oz) fish stock

50g (2 oz) butter

75g (3 oz) tomato concasse, diced

8 tomato petals

METHOD

Cook the sweet potato until it just begins to break down and season with salt and pepper. Mix with 50g (2oz) of shallots and the chives and quenelle onto the tomato petals. Pan fry the salmon medallion and place resting on the sweet potato mash. Cook the sugar snaps, season and place on the tomato petals.

To make the sauce, sweat the remaining shallots, add the fish stock and reduce by two-thirds. Add the tomato grain mustard and spring onions, cut into fine lozenges. Shake in the butter and add the créme fraiche and sauce over the salmon.

LAMB HOTPOT WITH FENNEL & DILL SODA SCONES

INGREDIENTS

HOTPOT

1 kg (2 lb 4 oz) diced leg or shoulder of lamb
500 g (1 lb 2 oz) carrots
650 ml (1 pint 3 fl oz) good lamb stock
250 ml (9 fl oz) red wine
50 g (2 oz) flour
2 tablespoons vegetable oil

500 g (1 lb 2 oz) onions
70 g (3 oz) tomato purée
1 bulb of fennel
75 g (3 oz) butter
Salt and pepper to taste

DILL SODA SCONES

250 g (9 oz) plain flour
150 ml (5 fl oz) milk
1 teaspoon dried dill, or 3 teaspoons of fresh

15 g (½ oz) baking powder
30 g (1 oz) margarine
Salt and pepper to taste

Oven - 170 °C, 325 F, Gas mark 3

METHOD

Hotpot - Heat the oil in a thick bottomed pan, lightly flour the cubes of lamb and fry over a fierce heat to colour. This may require 2 or 3 batches. Place in a colander to drain.

Pour any excess oil from the pan and sweat the onions, carrots and fennel in the butter for 3 or 4 minutes with a lid. Add the tomato purée and cook out until it deepens in colour, mix in the flour and cook for a further 2 or 3 minutes.

Add the red wine, lamb stock and lamb to the pan. Bring to the boil, stirring occasionally. Season with salt and milled pepper and cook in the oven for 1½-2 hours.

Soda Scones - Sift the flour, baking powder and salt. Rub in the margarine and add the dill. Pour in the milk and mix together by hand. (The secret to success is to handle the dough as little and as lightly as possible.)

Turn the dough onto a floured surface and roll into 12 balls approximately 35 g (1½ oz) in weight. Flour the ball of your hand and simply press down to flatten to about 5 cm (2 inches) thick. Cook in one of two ways :

1. My first choice - Griddle on a traditional girdle or heavy-based frying pan for about 4-5 minutes on each side, or until golden brown and cooked in the centre. Cover with a damp cloth and then serve on top of the lamb hotpot.

2. Place on top of the hotpot (just overlapping), lightly brush with milk and continue to cook in the oven for 12 minutes.

WHISKY & HONEY BASE WITH GINGER BERRIES

INGREDIENTS

40g (1½ oz) fresh raspberries

40g (1½ oz) fresh strawberries

50ml (1 miniature) whisky, preferably malt

20g (¾ oz) fine oatmeal

48g (2 oz) ginger biscuits

10g (½ oz) preserved ginger

20g (¾ oz) fresh blueberries

40g (1½ oz) fresh blackberries

30g (1 oz) clear honey

200ml (7 fl oz) heavy cream

4 fresh mint leaves

80g (3 oz) caster sugar

METHOD

Reserve a few berries for garnish and place the remaining berries with the sugar and 10ml of the whisky into a bowl. Gently mix, but do not crush the fruit. Chop the ginger into small pieces and add to the fruit. Leave for 30 minutes. Toast the oatmeal and leave to cool. Whip the cream with the honey and remaining whisky. Crush the ginger biscuits and with the oatmeal fold into the cream. Spoon the fruit into tall glasses, then pipe on some of the cream and repeat twice more to get a layered effect. Garnish the tops with mint leaf and a few berries. Serve with an extra ginger biscuit, if desired.

NO: 123] SUMMER MENU (SERVES FOUR)

RAYMOND BLANC

EXECUTIVE HEAD CHEF, LE MANOIR AUX QUAT' SAISONS, OXFORD

GRILLED SUMMER VEGETABLES

INGREDIENTS

2 courgettes, cut lengthways into 3 mm slices

1 red pepper, skinned, halved, seeded, each half cut in two

Salt and freshly ground black pepper

1 aubergine, cut widthways into 5 mm (1/4 inch) slices

2 tomatoes, skinned, halved and seeded

2 tablespoons balsamic vinegar

MARINADE

100 ml (3 1/2 fl oz) extra virgin olive oil

4 sprigs of fresh thyme or a large pinch of dried thyme

2 garlic cloves, peeled and sliced

6 fresh basil leaves

Marinating time - 6-12 hours

METHOD

Mix all the prepared vegetables with the ingredients of the marinade. Stir so they are coated with the olive oil. Cover with cling film and marinate at room temperature for 6-12 hours.

Place in a ridged cast-iron grill pan (or on a barbecue) and brush with the marinade. Place on medium heat and cook the courgettes and tomatoes for 2 minutes on each side and the aubergines and peppers for 4 minutes on each side.

To finish, taste and season with salt and pepper. Place on a serving dish and sprinkle with the balsamic vinegar.

BEST END OF LAMB WITH A HERB CRUST

"The French do not know how to cook lamb!"

INGREDIENTS

1 tablespoon olive oil

Salt and freshly ground black pepper

200 ml (7 fl oz) water

1 best end of lamb, about 8 ribs, perfectly trimmed

2 tablespoons Dijon mustard

BREADCRUMB COATING

110 g (4 oz) dried breadcrumbs, not too finely ground

1 teaspoon dried thyme

2 tablespoons olive oil

1 tablespoon chopped fresh parsley

1/2 teaspoon chopped fresh rosemary needles

Fennel purée

1/2 quantity braised fennel with cardamom

90 ml (3 fl oz) extra virgin olive oil

Oven - 230 °C, 450 F, Gas Mark 8

METHOD

To make the breadcrumb coating, mix all the dry ingredients together, then add the olive oil. Mix to a sandy texture and reserve on a small tray.

Cook the fennel and allow to cool. Purée in a liquidiser, adding the olive oil gradually. Taste and season.

Pre-heat the oven. In a small roasting pan, heat the olive oil and sear and colour the lamb on all sides for about 5 minutes. Add and sear the small chopped chine bones at the same time. Season with salt and pepper. Place the lamb on to the chine bones, so it does not touch the bottom of the pan, and roast in the oven for about 10 minutes.

Remove the lamb from the oven and spread mustard all over the meat part (not the bones). Press the meat into the breadcrumbs until it is completely coated. Roast for a further 12-15 minutes in the oven.

To make the juice, remove the lamb from the oven and reserve on a small plate for about 8-10 minutes, loosely covered with foil.

Remove most of the fat from the roasting pan and add the water. Scrape off the caramelised bits, stirring all the bones around and simmer for 5 minutes until you obtain 100 ml (3½ fl oz) of juice. Strain and keep warm.

Gently re-heat the fennel purée. You can either carve the lamb in front of your guests or do it in the privacy of your kitchen. Serve the purée and lamb juice separately.

BRAISED FENNEL WITH CARDAMON

INGREDIENTS

500 g (18 oz) baby fennel bulbs, or large bulbs cut into 4 or 6, according to size

50 ml (2 fl oz) extra virgin olive oil

2 garlic cloves, peeled and sliced

2 sprigs of fresh thyme

4 black olives, stoned

3 cardamon pods, lightly crushed

500 ml (17 fl oz) water

Salt and freshly ground white pepper

METHOD

Pre-heat the oven to 180 °C 350 F Gas Mark 4.

Sweat the fennel for about 10 minutes in the olive oil in a flameproof casserole. Add the garlic, thyme, black olives, cardamon and water or stock. Season with salt and pepper. Bring to the boil, cover with a lid then cook in the pre-heated oven for 1½-2 hours. Serve to your guests.

VARIATIONS

The fennel can be served whole, as a vegetable, but it can also be puréed, to serve as a vegetable purèe (good with lamb), or as a sauce (good with red mullet).

Chef's notes

The best olives are the ones in olive oil with Provençal herbs.
The ones kept in brine are not so tasty.

The sweating of the fennel will remove its coarse taste and extract
the sugar. Do not colour.

The cooking time for the fennel may seem very long, but it is essential
to cook it thoroughly so a proper exchange of flavours can take place.

POACHED WHITE PEACHES WITH ORANGE SABAYON & WILD STRAWBERRIES

INGREDIENTS

PEACHES

700 ml bottle dry white wine

1/2 vanilla pod

4 lemon slices, 5 mm (1/4 inch) thick, skin included

1 disk of greaseproof paper to fit the diameter-

-of your stainless steel saucepan

120 g (41/2 oz) caster sugar

4 orange slices, 5 mm (1/4 inch) thick, skin included

4 ripe peaches, about 150 g (5 oz) each

SABAYON

2 egg yolks

1 tablespoon Grand Marnier

50 ml (2 fl oz) whipping cream

STRAWBERRIES

80 g (31/4 oz) wild strawberries (or strawberries)

1 teaspoon caster sugar

A dash of lemon juice

METHOD

In a stainless-steel saucepan, bring the wine, sugar, vanilla pod, orange and lemon slices to the boil. When boiling, add the peaches, cover with the greaseproof paper disk, and bring back to the boil. Simmer for 4-5 minutes.

Remove from the heat and leave the peaches to cool in their cooking juices until at room temperature. Carefully place in a suitable container and reserve in a refrigerator until required.

To make the sabayon, in a medium saucepan, bring to the boil 300 ml (10 fl oz) of the peach juices, then lower the heat. Allow the juice to reduce gently to 100 ml (31/2 fl oz).

While the juice is reducing, place the egg yolks into an electric mixer bowl, ready to be beaten. You can also whip the cream up to soft peaks in a separate bowl and reserve in a refrigerator.

When the juice has reduced to the correct volume, switch the electric mixer on to its highest speed and carefully pour the boiling juice on to the egg yolks in between the side of the bowl and the beaters. Beat until completely cold. Remove the cream from the refrigerator and fold it delicately into the yolk and syrup mixture along with the Grand Marnier. Cover with cling film and reserve in a refrigerator.

Place the wild strawberries, sugar and lemon juices in a bowl and shake the bowl gently to coat the fruit completely. Allow them to marinate for up to 1 hour.

To serve, drain the peaches from their remaining juices and skin them. Quarter each peach and very carefully remove each quarter from the stone. Arrange four quarters in a glass, and spoon equal quantities of the sabayon on top. Sprinkle over the marinated wild strawberries and serve.

NO:124] AUTUMN MENU (SERVES FOUR)

MICHEL FLAMME

EXECUTIVE HEAD CHEF, THE KILDARE HOTEL & COUNTRY CLUB, STRAFFAN, COUNTY KILDARE, IRELAND

ROASTED SCALLOPS WITH A COMPÔTE OF ONION & CHIVES & BELGIAN ENDIVE

INGREDIENTS

8 large scallops

1 large Spanish onion

110 g (4 oz) butter

10 g (1/2 oz) chives, chopped

8 slices streaky bacon, crispy

1 1/2 tablespoons oil

2 Belgian endives, cooked

Butter for sautéing

Thyme

1 clove

570 ml (1 pint) chicken stock

Salt and pepper

"BLANC"

1 1/4 litres (2 pints) water

225 g (8 oz) flour

1 lemon juice

METHOD

Cook the Belgian endive in a "Blanc" for 35 minutes, which allows the endives to stay white. Roll them tightly in cling film.

Slice the onions, sweat on a low heat for 20 minutes in butter until tender. Add the clove and thyme and pour on the chicken stock. Cook slowly until the liquid has evaporated. Liquidise and finish by adding half the measured butter (55 g, 2 oz), seasoning and the chives.

Pan fry the scallops in 55 g (2 oz) butter and the oil. During the cooking time, turn them often and baste with a spoon. They need to be dark brown but very soft inside. Put the bacon under the grill until crispy.

To serve, put four spots of onion compôte on a plate and add two scallops and the crispy bacon.

Top with long pieces of thin chives.

CUTLET OF PORK WITH ARTICHOKE & OLIVE, BAY LEAF JUS

INGREDIENTS

4 globe artichokes

50 g (2 oz) black olives, stoned

175 ml (6 fl oz) veal jus

2 sprigs thyme

10 g (½ oz) Parma ham trimming

110 g (4 oz) butter

Oven - 180 °C, 350 F, Gas Mark 4

50 g (2 oz) olive oil

75 ml (3 fl oz) white wine

3 garlic cloves

2 bay leaves

2 x 350 g (12 oz) pork cutlets

METHOD

Sweat the artichoke in olive oil for 5 minutes. Add the Parma ham trimming and sweat for another 5 minutes. Add the white wine, garlic, thyme, olive, bay leaves and stock and cook in the oven for 25 minutes. Cover with tin foil.

Pan fry the pork cutlets until cooked, basting often. Take off the bone. On a plate put the artichoke stew and finish with a slice of pork with "garende" salt and the sauce.

CARAMELIZED JOHN O' GOLD

INGREDIENTS (PER SERVING)

1 John O' Gold apple

1 cinnamon stick

1 small red apple

Ice cream

Oven - See text below

75 g (3 oz) sugar

110 g (4 oz) puff pastry

(to make this yourself see section on handy basics)

METHOD

Roll out the puff pastry to ¼ cm thick. Place in a refrigerator and allow to rest for 1 hour. Remove from the refrigerator and prick with a fork. Cook in a hot oven, 230 °C, 450 F, Gas Mark 6, for 12-15 minutes or until golden brown and flaky. Set aside to cool. Once the pastry has cooled, cut rounds for the base of the dessert using a 5 cm (2 inch) round cutter. Dust with icing sugar and place under a grill until the sugar has caramelised. Repeat on the other side.

Caramelise the sugar in a heavy-bottomed pan until a rich dark syrup is produced. Halve the apple, peel, core and cut into 8 segments. Place in the caramel, toss and allow to cook until soft.

Slice the small red apple very thinly and place on a non-stick tray. Sprinkle with icing sugar. Reduce the temperature of the oven to 200 °C, 400 F, Gas Mark 6. Place the apple chips in the oven for 5 minutes, or until golden brown.

To serve, place the puff pastry in a 5¾ cm (2¼ inch) salad ring, 4 cm (1½ inch) high. Pack the apple into the ring, turn onto the serving plate and remove the ring. Place apple chips on top and garnish with ice cream.

NO: 125] WINTER SUPPER (SERVES SIX)

THE LATE LINDA MCCARTNEY
SINGER, PHOTOGRAPHER & AUTHOR OF VEGETARIAN COOKBOOKS

PASTA & BEAN SALAD WITH BASIL & PECORINO

"An alluring mixture of bell peppers, green beans and kidney beans, pasta and herbs, this salad's finishing touch is finely pared cheese. It's really a meal in itself, served with warm fresh bread."

INGREDIENTS

SALAD

1 red bell pepper

175 g (6 oz) green beans, cooked

4 dessertspoons chopped parsley

50 g (2 oz) pecorino romano cheese, pared finely into shavings

225 g (8 oz) bow-tie pasta

1 yellow bell pepper

200 g (7 oz) red kidney beans, tinned or cooked and dried

A handful of fresh basil leaves, shredded

SOY AND LEMON DRESSING

3-4 tablespoons soy sauce

Freshly ground black pepper, to taste

1 garlic clove, minced

Juice of 1 lemon

6 tablespoons dark sesame oil

1 teaspoon grated fresh ginger

METHOD

Dressing - Mix all the ingredients together in a small bowl.

Salad - Cut the peppers into quarters and seed. Cut each quarter into 2 or 3 strips and place skin-side up under a hot grill. Grill for 5-6 minutes or until the skin has blistered and blackened. Remove, place in a brown paper bag and cool. The skin will peel off easily. Cut the peppers into thin slices.

Cook the pasta in boiling water until "al dente" Drain and rinse immediately under cold water in a colander.

Mix the peppers, pasta, green beans, kidney beans and parsley in a salad bowl. Add the dressing and toss until thoroughly mixed together. Finally, fold in the basil and garnish with the pecorino shavings.

WINTER LASAGNE

"One of the joys of this dish is that it is so easy to prepare. It can also be made well in advance and then put into the oven when you are ready to cook it."

INGREDIENTS

350 g (12 oz) mushrooms, sliced

700 g (1¹/₂ lb) vegetarian mince meat

800 g (1³/₄ lb) tinned tomatoes or 575 g (1¹/₄ lb) fresh tomatoes, skinned and chopped

Sea salt and freshly ground black pepper, to taste

A sprinkling of dried mixed herbs of your choice

225 g (8 oz) lasagne, cooked until "al denté"

450 g (1 lb) fresh spinach, cooked and drained well, then chopped

150 g (5 oz) grated cheese

5 tablespoons vegetable oil

1 onion, chopped

Minced garlic, to taste

Béchamel sauce, see p. 169

2 free range eggs, beaten

Oven - 190 °C, 375 F, Gas Mark 5

METHOD

Sauté the mushrooms briskly in 3 tablespoons of hot oil until they are lightly cooked and crisp. Set aside. Mix the vegetarian mince with the chopped onion and cook in the rest of the oil until the onion softens a little, 4-5 minutes.

Cover the bottom of a baking dish with chopped tomatoes and season with salt and pepper, garlic and a sprinkling of herbs. Cover with the lasagne strips and make the next layer with the mince mixture. Season again. Spread the spinach on top and then the mushrooms. Continue making layers, finishing with a layer of lasagne.

Heat the béchamel gently and stir in the grated cheese until it melts. Remove from the heat and stir in the beaten eggs. Pour over the top of the lasagne and bake in a pre-heated oven until well-browned on top, for about 1 hour.

BÉCHAMEL SAUCE

INGREDIENTS

4 tablespoons butter or margarine
500 ml (17 fl oz) skimmed or soy milk, warmed
Sea salt and freshly ground black pepper

3 tablespoons flour
A pinch of grated nutmeg

METHOD

Melt the butter in a small, heavy-bottomed saucepan. Gradually stir in the flour, using a wooden spoon. Add the warm milk slowly, stirring all the time until the sauce thickens. Season to taste with nutmeg, salt and pepper and simmer over a very low heat for 5-6 minutes.

FLOATING ISLANDS

"No one can resist this dessert of tender poached meringue 'islands' floating on a custard 'sea'. The custard is stabilised with cornflour, which will prevent any curdling."

INGREDIENTS

850 ml (1½ pint) milk
125 g (4½ oz) caster sugar
½ teaspoon salt
Raspberry jelly

3 free range eggs, separated
1 tablespoon cornflour
½ teaspoon vanilla or almond extract-
-or ¼ teaspoon apple pie spice (nutmeg/cinnamon)

METHOD

Heat the milk in a wide saucepan. Meanwhile, put 2 of the egg whites in a bowl and beat until frothy. Add 2 tablespoons of the sugar and beat until stiff.

Drop large heaped spoonfuls of the egg whites onto the hot milk, to make 6 or 8 meringues. Poach gently until the meringues feel just firm to the touch, turning them over so that they are cooked on both sides. When they are ready, remove with a slotted spoon and drain on paper towels.

Combine the remaining sugar, cornflour and salt in a bowl and stir to mix. Add the remaining egg white and yolks and mix together until smoothly blended. Pour in the hot milk, stirring. Pour the custard mixture into the top of a double boiler set over simmering water, or into a heavy-based saucepan and cook until thickened, stirring constantly. Remove from the heat and cool slightly, then stir in the extract or spice. Pour the custard into a wide serving dish and let it cool completely.

Before serving, arrange the meringues on top of the custard and dot with raspberry jelly.

St. George's Crypt-
a lifeline to many!

Quotes from women visiting the Family Centre

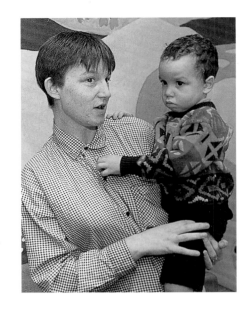

Crisis

' Because of my husband's violence, my children and I left home without anything. The Centre provided us with food and clothes. '

Father Christmas:

' My husband lost his job just before Christmas. Our children wouldn't have had any new toys but for the Crypt. '

Friendship:

' Coming to the Centre stops me being lonely. Staff take time to listen to me and I can talk over my problems with them. '

Stability:

' Coming here has helped me get back on my feet after a bad time. '

Acceptance:

' The people at the Crypt are my family. '

We hope that you and your family enjoy using this cookbook.

Should you wish to help those who don't know where their next meal will come from, or in whose company it will be eaten, send this page with a donation to:

> Professor D F Goldspink
> 'More Than a Roof' Project Co-ordinator
> St George's Crypt
> Great George Street
> LEEDS LS1 3BR
> Telephone: 0113 245 9061   Facsimile: 0113 244 3646

☐ I enclose a donation of £＿＿＿＿＿＿＿＿
Please make cheques payable to 'More Than a Roof'

☐ I would like to donate £ ＿＿＿＿＿＿＿ via my ☐ credit card or ☐ charity card

Credit Card is ＿＿＿＿＿＿＿＿＿＿＿＿＿ eg Visa, Mastercard

Card No ＿＿＿＿＿＿＿＿＿＿＿＿＿＿＿＿

Expiry Date ＿＿＿＿＿＿＿＿＿＿＿＿

Signature ＿＿＿＿＿＿＿＿＿＿＿＿＿＿＿＿＿＿＿＿ Date ＿＿＿＿＿＿＿＿＿

☐ Please send me a Gift Aid form (minimum Gift Aid donation = £250)
This enables the charity to claim 25% tax on top of your donation

☐ I would like a covenant form to spread my giving over 4 years
Tax can be reclaimed if you are a wage earner

If the amount raised by the appeal is greater than the cost of the redevelopment we propose to allocate any surplus to the day to day running costs of the Charity.

☐ Please tick this box if you would find this acceptable when making a donation

☐ I would like more information on your 'More Than a Roof' appeal

Name ＿＿＿＿＿＿＿＿＿＿＿＿＿＿＿＿＿＿＿＿＿＿＿

Address ＿＿＿＿＿＿＿＿＿＿＿＿＿＿＿＿＿＿＿＿＿＿＿＿＿＿＿＿＿＿

＿＿＿＿＿＿＿＿＿＿＿＿＿＿＿＿＿＿＿＿ Post Code ＿＿＿＿＿＿＿＿＿

☐ Please tick if you require an acknowledgement/receipt

We look forward to hearing from you and thank you in advance for your support.